The Logistics of Literacy Intervention

AN RTI PLANNING GUIDE FOR ELEMENTARY SCHOOLS

by Joanne Klepeis Allain, MA

Sopris West®
EDUCATIONAL SERVICES

A Cambium Learning® Company

BOSTON, MA · LONGMONT, CO

ISBN-13: 978-1-60218-815-0
ISBN-10: 1-60218-815-7
JDE #: 173921/11-10

Printed in the United States of America
Published and Distributed by

Sopris West®
EDUCATIONAL SERVICES

A Cambium Learning® Company

4093 Specialty Place • Longmont, Colorado 80504
(303) 651-2829 • www.sopriswest.com

ABOUT THE AUTHOR

Joanne Klepeis Allain received her master's degree in secondary curriculum and instruction from California State Polytechnic University in 1998. Her tenure in education has focused on at-risk youth, specifically adolescents who struggle to read. Joanne served for many years at both the classroom and district levels for the Los Angeles County Office of Education, Alternative Education Programs, whose target population includes students expelled from school. The literacy challenges presented by Joanne's students led to her interest and study in the field of adolescent literacy.

Joanne has served as a graduate-level instructor for California State Polytechnic University and the University of California–Los Angeles. She served as a national trainer for *LANGUAGE!® The Comprehensive Literacy Curriculum* and was named Trainer of the Year in 2005. Joanne has presented at national and international conferences that focus on the needs of at-risk youth and the educational systems that serve them.

Joanne is currently in private practice as a literacy consultant with 3t Literacy Group, focusing on implementation of literacy intervention for districts, states, and schools across the country. She resides in Long Beach, Calif., with her husband and two Redbone hounds, Leon and Lizzie.

To inquire about literacy intervention planning at your school or district, email Joanne at Joanne.Allain@3tliteracygroup.com or www.3tliteracygroup.com.

DEDICATION

For Jim, my best friend, mentor, and spouse, who taught me never to begin business without a few flowers.

Four Year-Old's First Test

You do a graceless swan dive
off the couch
when the new woman appears
to test you for kindergarten.
After you have shown her
your hockey trophy, your sister's photograph,
she begins
with authority:
"How are a pencil and a crayon similar?"
You say, "They are both skinny."
She checks the box marked wrong.
"Fill in the blank—red, white, and … "
"Green." Wrong again.
"Where does ham come from?"
You think and think
then say, "God."
Wrong.
"What would someone who is brave do?"
You answer quickly,
"Walk through rose bushes."

—*Christine Lamb Parker*

CONTENTS

Introduction

As educators, we continually strive to improve the way we educate our children. It is our goal to ensure that all students leave us able to negotiate a complex world. We want all of our students to have choices in life and to ultimately make the world a safer, saner place. Those of us in the schools of America recognize the difficult tasks that lay ahead of us. Yet, we do not shrink from our calling. We, above all others, recognize that children are our future.

Elementary education has undergone significant changes in the last ten years. Some would say we are seeing the pendulum of education swing once again. Debates about the best way to teach reading still exist. However, the focus on elementary students, I believe, has brought us to a place in which we are analyzing our educational process and designing structural and instructional programs that are based on reading research and proven instructional design. Regardless of our philosophical stance on reading instruction, we can all agree that our students—not personal preferences—must be the focus of everything we do.

WHAT WE KNOW

The components necessary to teach early reading have been identified in current scientifically based reading research (SBRR), which is defined as using "rigorous, systematic, and objective procedures to obtain knowledge about reading development, reading instruction, and reading difficulties. This type of reading research involves controlled experiments with data analysis and a thorough peer-review process" (Reading First, 2007). Based on this research, The Report of the National Reading Panel (2000) defined five essential components that make up SBRR instruction: phonemic awareness, phonics, fluency, vocabulary, and comprehension. Explicit and systematic instruction of these skills provide the basis for quality reading programs throughout the country and are reflected in federal and state regulations, grants, and mandates.

Reading First is a federal program that was originally authorized as part of the No Child Left Behind Act that was signed into law in January, 2002. The purpose is to ensure that every child reads at or above grade level by the end of third grade. The initiative contains requirements in four major components (www.readingfirstsupport.us):

1. Instructional programs and strategies, which contain scientifically based instructional content

SBRR

1

that explicitly and systematically address the five essential components of reading instruction—phonemic awareness, phonics, fluency, vocabulary, and comprehension—which were identified by the National Reading Panel in 2000.

2. Valid and reliable assessments that measure students progress in the five essential components of reading. The types of assessments include: screening assessments, diagnostic assessments, classroom-based assessments, and outcome assessments.

3. Professional development that is designed to increase student achievement by increasing teacher effectiveness in the delivery of scientifically based reading instruction.

4. Instructional leadership that includes clearly defined roles and responsibilities for district and school administrators to enable them to successfully implement a comprehensive reading program. me

As a result, many state educational agencies and their districts have adopted Reading First criteria and rigorously seek to ensure that the tenets of the program are implemented as designed.

In 2004, the Individuals with Disabilities Education Act was reauthorized. It brought focus to the growing practice of Response to Intervention (RtI) as an alternative to using a discrepancy formula to identify students who have learning disabilities. "RtI is the practice of providing high-quality instruction and interventions matched to student need, monitoring progress frequently to make decisions about changes in instruction or goals, and applying child-response data to important educational decisions" (Batsche, et al., 2007, p. 3). RtI is based on the premise that all students should receive high-quality initial instruction based on scientific reading research along with interventions targeted to their specific need before being referred to special education. It is essentially an all-education initiative in which referral to special education is the last resort, not the first. RtI requires the collaboration, cooperation, and coordination of the entire instructional staff. In effect, all students become our students. We label the need, not the child. The National Association of State Directors of Special Education (NASDSE) (Batsche, et al.) identifies three tiers of instruction in an elementary RtI process:

- Tier 1: initial instruction and differentiation that is scientifically based and has a high probability of teaching most students to read.

- Tier 2: targeted, intensive, short-term intervention for students who are not responding adequately to Tier 1 instruction.

- Tier 3: intensive intervention administered for a longer time period for students who do not respond to either Tier 1 or Tier 2 instruction, which may or may not include special-educational services.

Kame'ennui (2007, p. 7) states, "… what the law (Individuals with Disabilities Education Act, 2004) makes transparent is that RtI is essentially and instrumentally an assessment and instructional process that is dynamic, recursive, and based on rigorous scientific research." Barbara Foorman (2007, pp. 26–27) provides an essential question that must be asked as we attempt to meet the needs of beginning readers: "The question to ask about beginning reading instruction, then, is not, 'what are best practices?' but rather, 'what instructional activities are appropriate for this student at this phase of his or her reading development to maximize achievement outcomes?'" Clearly, we are moving from a generic application of using one level of reading instruction for all elementary children to an instruction and intervention model that requires targeted assistance as soon as students begin to struggle.

Still to be determined is what an RtI model looks like in urban and rural schools as well as in large and small schools. States and districts have various interpretations of the number of instructional tiers and what the appropriate instruction is for each. Some educational institutions identify Tier 3 as special education, while others design Tier 3 to include all students performing significantly below grade level, whether or not they are receiving special-education services. Agencies also vary in how they equate tiers of instruction to federal, state, and local performance categories. In general, students who are performing at or above grade level receive Tier 1 instruction. Students who are in need of additional assistance provided by Tier 2 instruction are performing slightly below grade level, and students who are in need of Tier 3 instruction are performing significantly below grade level. Regardless of the number of instructional tiers a state, district, or school adopts, we must plan for all students and all configurations.

One of many important questions for elementary schools is how and when students are identified as needing additional instruction. The RtI model may differ in grades K–3 and grades 4–5. For example, one model of RtI recommends the use of universal screening with five weeks of progress monitoring before referring students to intervention and then discontinuing intervention when students have shown significant progress (Fuchs & Fuchs, 2007). The rationale behind this model suggests that if universal screening for reading difficulties is the only measure applied, too many students may be identified as needing intervention when quality initial instruction in Tier 1 may resolve the issue. With beginning readers, we may have little historical performance data to inform placement in an instructional tier, so referral to intervention demands fluidity. However, in grades 4–5 we usually have historical performance data that may call for a different identification process. Should we restrict fourth- and fifth-grade students to Tier 1 instruction when data shows that they have been chronically performing below grade level? Even if a school were to retool its Tier 1 instruction across all elementary grades, the new curriculum will not fill the holes created by inadequate instruction that may have already occurred in grades K–3. If we are acting in the best interest of the child, it stands to reason that we intervene as soon as we know he/she is struggling and we are reasonably certain that core instruction (Tier 1) will not solve the problem. Kame'ennui (2007, p. 7) states, " … because RtI is ripe in the current discourse and practice of the profession, the implementation of RtI at the child, classroom, school, and district levels will be decidedly varied in form, process, and technical substance."

It is imperative that elementary schools take notice and embrace an RtI model as the foundation of their instructional program. Recent results from the National Assessment of Educational Progress (2007) inform us that, although we have made some gains from 2005, an unacceptable percentage of students are still struggling to read. According to the 2007 Nation's Report Card, 44% of all students in fourth grade are performing below basic levels in reading. Fifty-four percent of African American students and 51% of Hispanic students are performing below basic levels, while 23% of white students are performing below basic levels. Even with all of the changes in elementary education, too many students are reading below grade level, and the achievement gap still prevails in our educational institutions.

WHAT ELSE CAN WE DO?

Reading First, the National Association of State Directors, and leading reading and school-reform researchers emphasize the importance of leadership and quality implementation in the adoption of comprehensive literacy reform in our elementary schools. Administrators have been trained and retrained, yet the actual implementation of scientifically based reading instruction and intervention still flounders. The discrepancy between training and implementation is often an explicit plan that brings the research and federal directives about reading instruction to the reality and unique composition of each school. Researchers identify the best practices and components necessary to teach the most students to read and give general and specific guidelines to accomplish this. Federal agencies, then, make laws and policies that reflect the best of that knowledge. In turn, states mandate practices and policies and create goals for school districts that align with federal law. Based on these mandates, school districts develop strategic plans to enact new directives. Schools are expected to implement those plans. However, each level of directive, model, and strategic plan is often too global to become a reality at the school site. Each school within a district is unique; therefore, a one-size-fits-all plan can prove to be a disappointment when implemented. When discussing what schools do when students do not learn, Dufour and colleagues (2004, p. 36) stated, "Each staff must develop its own plan for meeting the needs of students in their unique school." I wholeheartedly support this statement, but would add that whatever plan the staff develops must be based on scientifically based reading instruction and intervention delivered in a fluid literacy system. Therefore, two types of plans must be developed within a district:

1. A district-wide plan that provides guidelines and includes non-negotiable criteria for reading instruction.
2. School-site plans that adhere to the district plan but reflect the uniqueness of the school site relative to practical implementation.

As an educational consultant, I have the privilege of observing and working with districts and schools attempting to develop the best model of reading instruction and intervention for their students. Clearly their intentions are pure. Many embrace and implement scientifically based reading instruction and work through the complexities of developing a viable RtI system. However, what I often see at the school site falls short of the district vision. District and site administrators and teachers continue to grapple with the everyday challenges of actual implementation. As a result of nonspecific plans, the goal of a fluid literacy instruction and intervention system morphs into a hit-and-miss instructional program. Examples of practical considerations at the school site include:

- What do we do when a new student arrives after the beginning of the school year?
- How do we report progress that includes progress toward state standards and reflects reading growth?
- How do we differentiate in Tier 1 with so many different levels in a class?
- How much time should students in Tiers 2 and 3 receive in addition to Tier 1 instruction?
- Should students in need of Tier 3 instruction receive a replacement curriculum?
- How are the needs of gifted students addressed in an RtI model?
- What if a school has a large number of students in need of strategic instruction (Tier 2)?

- What factors, besides student data, should be considered when moving a student from one tier to another?
- Who should teach each tier?
- How much training should be provided to the teacher, administrator, and support staff? Who should provide it?
- What happens when a teacher is hired midyear?

These questions and resulting frustrations may seem like minutia. However, it is exactly this lack of realistic foresight that impedes effective implementation of systemic literacy reform at the school site.

Assisting schools to resolve these issues while working through the logistical issues of everyday school life resulted in the development of *Logistics of Literacy Intervention: An RtI Planning Guide for Elementary Schools*. It is an effort to assist districts and elementary schools who are either beginning the process of RtI or are having difficulties with current implementation of RtI. The difficulty lies in bringing together the research from the literacy and school-reform communities and interpreting and applying that knowledge in the real-world setting of each district and school. It is not a one-size-fits-all planning process, but rather, it provides challenges, questions, and possible solutions for the everyday obstacles that face our schools. The ultimate purpose of Logistics of Literacy Intervention is to guide districts and schools to develop precise, practical RtI plans unique to their configuration, population, and community. These policies and procedures will be codified and organized into a district and/or school-site handbook that will serve to address the everyday concerns of teachers and administrators. *goals*

In order to provide a succinct organization for the process planning of an RtI system, organization of Logistics of Literacy Intervention follows the three phases of school reform developed by Michael Fullan (2001):

1. **Initiation:** the process that results in the decision to move forward with comprehensive literacy reform based on an RtI model.
2. **Implementation:** the process of putting an RtI model into practice, which can span from one to three years. *Get this established.*
3. **Continuance:** the process that results in the institutionalization of an RtI system that can withstand changes in funding, configuration, and personnel.

So, ask yourself the hard questions, don't be afraid of the answers, and let the planning begin. Our students are waiting for us!

Initiation

PHASE 1: *Initiation*

Fullan (2001) describes the process of initiation as the period in which an innovation or improvement project is adopted or a decision is made to move forward to achieve a desired goal. Applied to an RtI model, initiation begins the moment that a state, district, or school recognizes the need to address their struggling readers and decides to act on that information. The initiation phase sets the stage for the quality of implementation and sustainability of effective literacy instruction. During this phase, educators develop a set of ideals, goals, and policies that will promote clarity and unity of purpose around what students should learn, how they should learn it, and how educational institutions and personnel must be organized to meet the needs of struggling readers (Hill & Cielo, 1998).

Once the institution decides to move forward, a series of events occur that will guide the development of a precise literacy plan designed to meet the needs of all students. Some of the decisions during this phase include: (1) the number of students in need of intervention and to what degree; (2) the number of students that can be served based on fiscal, physical, and human resources; (3) how a large-scale RtI system will impact the school system and staff; and (4) how to build an efficient accountability system to measure the progress of students, teachers, the administrators, and the plan itself.

The following sections provide guidance for the state, district, or school that is either ready to begin a system of intervention or needs to rethink their current plan. It is a time to ask questions and develop answers, for it is the hard questions that make us recognize our students and ourselves on the road to improvement.

Setting Priorities

THE CHALLENGE

Millions of elementary students are reading below proficient levels in the United States (Individuals with Disabilities Education Act, 2005). We know that early reading instruction is crucial to school success; however, we must also acknowledge that there are many other needs at the school site. District administrators and school principals are under pressure to meet the acquisition of standards, adequate yearly progress goals, state growth goals, and the needs of English-language learners (ELLs) and special-education students. They are also expected to close the achievement gap; maintain safe schools; develop intervention plans; and meet the physical education, nutrition, social, and emotional needs of children. Just when districts and schools think they have everything under control, a new administration rolls into town demanding a shift in focus. How do we determine the priority level of one goal against the other when each one is of value? Our heads spin just thinking about it!

THE SOLUTION

The ultimate goal of the educational system is to produce students who are literate and able to participate in a democratic society. This is the primary goal for all students, not just our high achievers. "The first thing to realize is that decreasing the gap between high and low performers—boys, girls, ethnic groups, poor, rich, special education—is crucial because it has so many social consequences" (Fullan, Hill, & Crevola, 2007, p. 45). If we agree with the preceding statement as well as those of reading researchers, such as Dr. Louisa Moats (2007, p. 24), who asserts that we can teach children to read if we start early and have sufficient time and instructional intensity, then we must also agree that there is no higher priority. The elementary grades are the golden opportunity to make a difference in a student's academic, social, and emotional life. Fullan (2001), however, doubts the sustainability of innovations, such as Response to Intervention (RtI), because rather than ranking innovations relative to student achievement, educational institutions view every innovation as the top priority, resulting in nothing being done well. This is understandable given the pressures for school performance. However, we must weigh those innovations relative to each other and to student achievement. Dufour and colleagues (2006, p. 20) state, "When something is truly a priority in an organization, people do not hope it happens, they develop and implement systemic plans to ensure that it happens."

> "The elementary grades are the golden opportunity to make a difference in a student's academic, social, and emotional life."

Remember, it is better to do one thing well than to do ten things poorly. As you work on this section, ask yourself, what happens to students if we do not prioritize literacy instruction and intervention? Are we willing to make RtI the foundation of our instructional program?

KEYS TO SUCCESS

- What percent of your students have historically required literacy intervention? Do you expect this trend to continue?
- Do you believe that students must be literate to meet (not access) grade-level standards?
- Will higher literacy rates result in higher achievement in all academic areas?
- Will literacy intervention help your school/district/state meet local, state, and federal goals?
- Are other school-improvement projects as directly linked to student achievement as literacy instruction?
- If we do not focus on the development of literacy skill, what happens to students when they matriculate to middle school and high school?
- How many other school/district goals will be affected if students read at a higher rate?
- How do your school initiatives affect each other?

THE WORKSHEET

Use Worksheet 1.1 to itemize current and pending improvement projects and to analyze their relative importance to sustained student achievement. List projects and analyze their potential effect(s) on each other and on district and school goals as they relate to student achievement. Rate the projects on a scale from 1 to 5 (5 being the highest). This activity serves as a catalyst for discussion about the priority of literacy intervention and will set the stage for the planning necessary to achieve that goal.

Worksheet 1.1 *Setting Priorities*

(sample)

Improvement Project	Improves student performance in all content areas	Improves likelihood of graduation from high school	Raises standardized test scores	Assists school to meet state and federal goals	Raises student self-esteem	Helps close the achievement gap	Progress can be measured
Literacy instruction and intervention							

Literacy RtI Leadership

THE CHALLENGE

District and school administrators are already overwhelmed with mandates, accountability measures, students, parents, and teachers. The capacity of the district and school support staff is stretched to the limit with administrative budget cuts resulting in increasing workloads. Simultaneously, many states and educational organizations are finally encouraging, even mandating, an RtI approach for all students. As a result, district and school administrators are charged with interpreting how broad federal and state goals of literacy intervention in an RtI model can be implemented in their district and/or school site. Even though literacy is a primary objective of the elementary system, never before have we had to think about developing a fluid system that serves each student based on individual need. The National Association of State Directors of Special Educa-

tion (Batsche, et al., 2007) recommends that districts and schools focus on a model of prevention of failure to ensure literacy of all students. The question of who is going to lead this effort becomes crucial to the successful planning and implementation of literacy instruction.

"It is crucial to choose individuals who possess the commitment and passion needed to help struggling readers from a research perspective that embodies high expectations rather than a feel-good philosophy."

THE SOLUTION

The goal of selecting a dynamic, knowledgeable point person and team to provide effective leadership in not only improving the literacy of all students, but also in steering the development of a precise and workable plan at every phase of the RtI process, is a daunting task. Leadership at the district level (school site teams are discussed in Phase 2: Implementation) requires a literacy or an RtI coordinator and committee who will guide and direct instructional improvement and implementation plans. The immense responsibility of interpreting literacy and school-reform research as well as the functional workings of an RtI system requires a dedicated position, not just another hat that a district administrator is required to wear. Dufour and colleagues (2006, p. 21) articulate the importance of selecting the right person for the job: "If a leader resonates energy and enthusiasm, an organization thrives; if a leader spreads negativity and dissonance, it flounders." In addition, the District Literacy RtI Committee must represent all stakeholders who will be affected by the adoption of a district-wide literacy system and should include district administrators, site administrators, teachers, parents, and union representatives. Equally important is the inclusion of representatives of various student populations, such as general education, special education (including school psychologists and speech language pathologists), and ELLs.

It is crucial to choose individuals who possess the commitment and passion needed to help struggling readers from a research perspective that embodies high expectations rather than a feel-good philosophy. Organizational and communication skills are essential. The leaders must understand the inherent challenges in implementing an effective RtI system (Batsche, et al., 2007) and develop practical plans to overcome them.

KEYS TO SUCCESS

1. Seek out a Literacy Intervention Coordinator and District Literacy RtI Committee members who:
   - Believe that all students want to, can, and deserve to be literate.
   - Are willing to carefully analyze the district's current literacy instruction model and realistically report what is working and what needs repair.
   - Support the literature of Reading First, the No Child Left Behind Act, and the RtI process.
   - Understand the workings, culture, and challenges of elementary education.
   - Are process aware but product oriented.
   - Demonstrate respect for, and elicit respect from, all members of the educational community.
   - Will bridge the territorialism that may exist among departments for the good of all students.
   - Possess knowledge and/or are willing to research, learn, and embrace current literacy research.
   - Are familiar with assessment instruments and data analysis as they pertain to an RtI process.
   - Demonstrate the ability to think of what could be rather than what is.
   - Are effective communicators and problem solvers.

2. Articulate District Literacy RtI Committee tasks, including but not limited to:
   - Interpret state and federal mandates to develop a workable plan for school sites.
   - Offer support and guidance as needed by school site administrators and teachers.
   - Develop goals and a literacy mission statement.
   - Determine the level(s) of student need within the elementary population.
   - Determine and secure funding for long-term implementation.
   - Review and recommend research-based instructional materials and strategies.
   - Develop an assessment system in accordance with the RtI model.
   - Develop accountability and support criteria for implementers.
   - Monitor administrator, teacher, and student progress at regular intervals.
   - Present progress reports before the school board.
   - Organize and present awareness sessions.
   - Organize initial and support training.

3. Prepare sample interview questions for potential candidates, such as:
   - Why is an RtI so important at the elementary level?

- What are the necessary components of literacy intervention for Tiers 1, 2, and 3?
- What qualities do you believe are necessary to be an effective literacy intervention teacher?
- If student scores are not showing progress, what steps would you take to identify the problem?
- What are the obstacles that elementary schools will face in implementing an RtI model? How would you overcome them?
- How would you respond if the school board wants to know how students will achieve at grade-level standards if they are spending time in intervention?
- How would you respond to a parent who wants an explanation of why their fourth grader is suddenly enrolled in intervention?
- What would you do if District Literacy RtI Committee members disagree about the type of instruction necessary for literacy intervention in Tiers 2 and 3?
- What steps would you take to resolve the problem that more than 50% of the elementary students at one school are not meeting benchmark in the first quarter?
- What steps should be taken if an administrator is openly opposed to the RtI system your district has adopted and does not support the mandate at his/her school?

THE WORKSHEETS

Worksheets 1.2a and 1.2b are guides to help you begin to assess the qualifications and qualities of a Literacy Intervention Coordinator and District Literacy RtI Committee candidates. Rate each candidate from 1 to 5 (5 being the highest) under each category. The worksheets are a starting point; they are not meant to be all-encompassing documents. Create similar rubrics that reflect the uniqueness of your district. Remember that good interview skills don't guarantee good performance. Always check candidates' credentials and references, and talk to their coworkers, supervisors, and subordinates.

Phase 1

Worksheet 1.2a *The District Literacy Coordinator Candidates*

Name of Candidate	Expertise in current reading research	Organizational skills	Communication skills	Knowledge of RtI systems	Additional comments or qualifications

Worksheet 1.2b *The District Literacy Intervention Committee Candidates*

Name of Candidate	Area of expertise and current position	Elementary Experience (Yes/No)	Organizational skills	Familiar with reading research and RtI systems	Communication skills	Familiar with assessment tools for reading	Additional comments or qualifications

Section 1.3

Mission and Goals

THE CHALLENGE

Many educational institutions develop literacy mission statements that portray their ideal school and depict an image about what its students should be able to do. This global statement usually contains phrases such as "life-long learners" or "able to compete in a global society." While this is an important part of strategic planning, principals and teachers are often left wondering how to realize the mission at the school site and in the classroom. The result of that confusion is that practitioners disregard the mission statement and it is left to decorate the administrative office of each district and school.

The major obstacle to adherence is that implementers (i.e., teachers and district and site administrators) view the mission as a superficial stab at doing the right thing. It is so vague that no one uses it as a focus in the classroom. In addition, lack of clarity about achieving the mission renders it useless. Dufour and colleagues (2006, p. 19) go as far as to say, "No school has ever improved simply because the staff wrote a mission statement." Additionally, Fullan (2001, p. 777) describes the notion of "false clarity" in which an innovation—in this case, RtI—is viewed as more of the same rather than a significant change that will require alterations in how a district or school assesses, instructs, and monitors students.

Schools are then required to develop goals that support a vague mission statement, which ultimately results in a set of hazy goals because no one knows how to accomplish the mission or what it means at the school site. Consequently, unattainable goals are created, such as "all students will read at grade level in one year." This is a wonderful notion but unlikely given the diversity of the skill levels of these students. If the goals are not attainable, it is unreasonable to expect that teachers and administrators will take them seriously.

THE SOLUTION

Instructional improvement around literacy requires that everyone understands the magnitude of the change and values the significance of its potential effect on student achievement. If literacy intervention in an RtI system is to succeed, everyone must have the same basic values and aims. Elmore (2000) describes this as "organizational coherence" and proposes that it is essential to creating an arena in which significant change can occur. This begins with a clearly stated mission followed by clear-cut planning at both district and school levels. In fact, Dufour and colleagues (2006, p. 19) contend that, "The words of a mission statement are not worth the paper they are written on unless people begin to *do* differently."

The word "mission" is defined as, "a particular task or goal assigned to a person or group" (The Oxford American Dictionary of Current English, 2002, p. 507). If we accept this definition, a literacy mission statement must be precise to the undertaken task. It is not global or vague. It is not something that will happen sometime in the future. It will happen now. It is the instructional charge on which districts and schools will develop their specific plans that will ultimately raise the achievement of their students. It defines RtI as the foundation of the elementary instructional program.

> *"If literacy intervention in an RtI system is to succeed, everyone must have the same basic values and aims."*

Sample 1

> *It is the mission of District/School X to provide scientifically based literacy instruction for all elementary students in order for them to compete academically and achieve at grade level. Schools will offer intervention to students exhibiting need, and teachers should differentiate instruction in grade-level classes.*

This is a lofty mission, but do we really know what this means at the classroom level? Is it so global that the implementation of this mission will not foster the coherence described by Elmore (2000)? Notice the words "offer" and "should." "Offer" implies that while schools will have something in place, not everyone needs to take advantage of it; and "should" is a verb of possibility. We never know if it actually happens. Planning around a mission such as this will result in disparity among schools.

Sample 2

> *It is the mission of District/School Y to assist all elementary students to achieve at grade level. All schools will adopt scientifically based reading instruction as defined by the National Reading Panel as their core curriculum. All students will be screened with valid and reliable reading assessments to determine areas of possible intervention and prevention. Students in grades K–2, who are performing up to two years below grade level will receive targeted intense intervention for 30 minutes per day in addition to grade-level instruction. Students in grades 3–5, who are performing up to two years below grade level, will receive targeted intense intervention for 30 minutes per day in addition to grade-level instruction. Students in grades 3–5, who are more than two years below grade level, will receive intense, explicit intervention in place of grade-level instruction.*

This mission statement provides clarity about the intentions of the district or school. It specifies a particular task that each school will perform. It is clear enough for districts and schools to build concise plans that will support the mission.

The goals developed to measure progress toward the mission must be rigorous yet reasonable. Think about the mission as the clear statement of intent, and the goals are benchmarks against which progress is measured. In *Raising Reading Achievement in Middle and High Schools*, Elaine K.

McKewan (2001, p. 11) provides the example of Lincoln School whose solely stated and measurable goal was to "reduce the number of students performing in the bottom quartile by ten percent." The goals we set for RtI must be embraced and attainable by all stakeholders. A charge of the District/School-Site Literacy RtI Committee is to set goals that can be enacted by all implementers, measured for progress, and revisited yearly for revision. Hill and Cielo (1998, p. 32) do an excellent job of explaining the importance of developing clear goals: "Schools that expect to make a major difference in what children know and can do have very clear goals, and they have definitive methods of pursuing these goals. The goals and methods color every transaction among faculty members and between faculty, students, parents, and other constituencies."

Goal setting is not for students alone. District/School-Site Literacy RtI Committees must set goals for themselves as well. In order for RtI to be successful, everyone must be accountable. Therefore, the committees must articulate group performance goals for the first and subsequent years as they progress toward achieving their mission, and review and revise those goals as needed.

KEYS TO SUCCESS

- Be clear and concise. This is not the place for flowery language. Remember you are describing a "particular task" that is being assigned to teachers and administrators.
- Do not use vague terms or verbs of possibility (e.g., should, could, might, may).
- Be realistic; the mission should reflect not only what you want to do but also what you can do.
- Make the mission statement clear. When developing the statement, think about the perception of the educators who will be implementing the mission.
- Consider consulting a professional to facilitate the articulation of a mission statement.
- The mission statement reflects the adoption of RtI as the foundation of your instructional program.

THE WORKSHEETS

Use Worksheet 1.3a to help you develop a literacy mission at the district or school site. Include all aspects of literacy instruction in a tiered model of delivery. Use Worksheets 1.3b–1.3e to help you develop goals for student progress and for the District/School-Site Literacy RtI Committee.

- Develop goals that are measurable and can be supported by funds, personnel, and materials.
- Articulate the evidence that will be required to ensure that the goal will be met.
- Develop realistic and attainable goals. Revisit and revise them yearly.
- Develop procedural goals as well as student-progress goals. Procedural goals include but are not limited to: professional development goals, school-site plans, materials and assessment identification, data collection, analysis and response, and observations and evaluation.

Worksheet 1.3a *District/School Vision and Literacy Mission Statement*

Brainstorm statements that reflect your district/school's intention relative to literacy:

Primary Objective:

Grade-level instruction (Tier 1):

_____

Targeted/strategic intervention (Tier 2):

_____

Intensive intervention (Tier 3):

_____

Use the previous statements to develop a literacy mission statement. Make sure the statement is clear and to the point.

Phase 1

Worksheet 1.3b *Student Progress Goals (Year 1)*

(sample)

Goal	Evidence	Achieved (Yes/No)	Response actions
Year 1			
5% fewer students will be identified at Tier 3.			
5% of students in Tier 2 will move to Tier 1 instruction.			
Literacy intervention students will show improvement on progress monitoring-assessment tools.			
Behavior referrals for literacy intervention students will decrease by 5%.			
Attendance of literacy-intervention students will improve by five days per year.			

Worksheet 1.3c *Student-Progress Goals (Years 1–3)*

Goal	Evidence	Achieved (Yes/No)	Response actions
Year 1			
Year 2			
Year 3			

Phase 1

Worksheet 1.3d *Literacy RtI Committee Sample (Year 1)*

(sample)

Sample goals	Lead person	Evidence	Due date	Notes
1. Develop a mission and student progress goals.				
2. Identify and administer a screening and diagnostic instrument to assess student need and placement.				
3. Train teachers to administer and evaluate screening and diagnostic assessments.				
4. Identify and validate research-based curricula for grade-level, strategic, and intensive students.				
5. Provide awareness sessions for administrators, teachers, counselors, and parents.				
6. Draft and present a literacy intervention resolution for adoption by the board of education.				
7. Draft a proposal in the performance plan of administrators and teachers to include progress of literacy-intervention students.				
8. Select and train teachers and administrators.				
9. Develop a template for schools to develop a school-site implementation plan.				
10. Order and distribute materials to school sites.				
11. Provide follow-up training for teachers and administrators throughout the year.				

Worksheet 1.3e *Literacy RtI Committee Goals (Year 1)*

Goals	Lead person	Evidence	Due date	Notes

Phase 1

Section 1.4

Funding

THE CHALLENGE

In a time of budget reductions and increasing mandates, identifying funds that can be dedicated to a long-term reform effort is a significant challenge. Each department within a district or school depends on targeted funds to support the goals of their respective populations, and they are not always willing to look at innovative or alternative methods to achieve these goals. Education seems to have a short attention span when it comes to adopting improvement projects. Often, thousands—even millions—of dollars are spent on materials, training, and coaching for innovations, such as literacy intervention, only to be abandoned in a few years for something newer or prettier that does the same job. Multiply this number by the three major populations in our schools (general education, special education, and ELLs) and we have wasted an unconscionable amount of money.

THE SOLUTION

The members of the District/School Literacy RtI Committee were chosen for two primary reasons: (1) expertise regarding their specific populations; and (2) to coordinate intellectual and funding resources for RtI planning, implementation, and continuation. An important aspect of this collaboration is to reduce the instructional and fiscal redundancy that occurs when each department attempts to achieve its primary goal for elementary education: literacy for all students. The NASDSE states, "While financial accountability is essential in the allocation of all public monies, harm can occur if programs with overlapping responsibilities are separated rigidly" (Batsche, et al., 2007, p. 9). The inclusive nature of the Literacy RtI Committee can serve to reduce the fiscal territorialism that currently exists among the departments representing our student populations. If students are assessed with similar needs, then funding from all sources can be used to achieve the primary goal. Therefore, it is important to identify all possible sources of funding and to determine what aspects of literacy instruction each source will cover. For example, one source of funding supports professional development for special education while another targets professional development for ELLs or general-education students. If the populations are blended within classes or programs, all financial sources may be utilized. We must seek to end the duplication that occurs in our schools. We cannot claim we have a seamless

"... it is important to identify all possible sources of funding and to determine what aspects of literacy instruction each source will cover."

instruction/intervention model if our programs and students are held hostage by withholding funds that could help all of them.

KEYS TO SUCCESS

- Research private- and public-funding sources geared toward reading instruction and RtI.
- Work with the parent organization as a possible fundraising source.
- Phone or email local, state, and federal consultants to see which funding sources would support literacy intervention. They will help you negotiate the language of funding requirements.
- Ask literacy intervention publishers if they are willing to work with the district on materials, training, or assessment. They need student-achievement data for validation of their curriculum.
- See if publishers have information on funding sources for districts interested in adopting a curriculum and if they are willing to help.
- Consult the grant writers at your district to apply for literacy grants.
- Consult the state and federal education agencies for grant opportunities.
- Include all possible funding sources for special education, general education, and ELLs.

THE WORKSHEETS

Use Worksheet 1.4a to assist in collecting information about various funding sources, specific amounts, and the designated criteria for spending. Use Worksheet 1.4b to help estimate possible costs that will arise as you go through the funding process. These worksheets serve as initial guidelines for allocated funds but can be altered to fit the uniqueness of your situation. Your district/ school may have additional revenue sources, costs, and concerns that are not listed.

Phase 1

Worksheet 1.4a *Literacy Intervention Funding Streams*

Funding	Fund type _____	Fund type _____	Fund type _____	Fund type _____	Total _____
Population (total amount available)					
Special education					
ELLs					
General education					
At-risk students					
Free and reduced lunch					
Primary (K–3)					
Intermediate (4–5)					
After-school programs					
Teachers					
Administrators					
Materials (total amount available)					
Teacher materials					
Student materials					
Classroom supplies					
Technology and technology support					
Professional Development (total amount available)					
Training room					
Audiovisual					
Food					
Substitute teachers					
Trainer fee					
Trainer expenses (e.g., airfare, meals, lodging)					
Follow-up training					
Coaches					
Administrator training					
Counselor training					
Data Collection (total amount available)					
Pre- and post-assessment materials					
Assessment administration and training					
Data collection					
Data analysis					
Technology for data collection					
TOTALS					

Worksheet 1.4b *Literacy Intervention Estimated Cost Sheet*

Item	Special education	ELLs	General education	Total cost	Funds available	Difference
Materials						
Student						
Teacher						
Training						
Administrator						
Supplies						
Technology and technology support						
Training						
Training fees						
Trainer expenses						
Training room						
Audiovisual						
Food						
Substitutes						
Administrator						
Teacher						
Paraprofessional						
Parents						
Follow-up						
Coaches						
Data Collection						
Materials						
Training						
Administration						
Collection						
Analysis						
Technology						
Personnel						

Phase 1

Section 1.5

Determining Need

THE CHALLENGE

Descriptions of seamless systems for RtI give the impression that most students are functioning at grade level, some students need strategic intervention, and fewer require intensive or Tier 3 instruction (Batsche, et al., 2007, p. 22). What happens if your school does not fit that model? What if the majority of students in the school are in need of Tier 2 or even Tier 3 instruction? What if many of the students entering kindergarten are ELLs or have low oral-language skills? How do we serve our proficient and advanced students in an RtI system?

Sometimes the sheer magnitude of student need can overwhelm district and school educators. Literacy committees must not only serve all students, but must also consider funding allocations, class schedules, and parent notification. Districts and schools may fear the political ramifications of identifying large numbers of struggling students. The current pressure placed on schools to have high percentages of students performing at proficient levels causes some schools and districts to underidentify struggling students. In other situations, district and school scores are high and the struggling student receives little or no additional instruction. Dr. Alex Granzin (2006) aptly expresses the immediacy of the issue: "Why don't we just stop everything when kids aren't learning to read? I mean, why are we even doing anything else? When kids don't master this process, why doesn't the red light start flashing immediately and say, 'Wait a minute, we're not moving on.' We're not going to treat this as though it is some sort of small problem that we can solve by sending you over here for a few extra minutes a day and possibly monitoring your progress a little bit more closely and hoping for the best." Most would agree with Dr. Granzin; but how do schools deal with other pressures that seem to make a comprehensive prevention/intervention system impossible?

The notion of such a system seems most intimidating for large elementary schools and year-round schools. How to create seamless prevention and intervention is not readily apparent in schools of 1,000 or more students or in multitrack elementary schools; rather, the task seems monumental. Many administrators feel frustrated because schools have no historical memory related to tiered instruction, and too often that results in denying these needs or creating a façade that looks good until it is closely examined. The truth is that every school has students who struggle, and they deserve to be literate.

THE SOLUTION

Rather than dismissing the RtI process, district/schools must recognize that elementary school is our best opportunity to address the academic achievement of our students so that we can send them to middle school ready to negotiate grade-level material. What begins with elementary students admitting, "I can't," can quickly change to, "I won't," in middle school. We want to prevent self-esteem issues as well as academic failure that will continue if not arrested in elementary school. The first step is to ascertain the configuration of each school within a district.

"What begins with elementary students admitting, 'I can't,' can quickly change to, 'I won't,' in middle school."

Figure 1.5 depicts three examples of RtI pyramids. In each pyramid, the lines are drawn to show variations of student skill. The first triangle shows that most students are performing at Tier 1, with some at Tier 2, and fewer at Tier 3. The second triangle shows that most students in a school are performing in Tier 2, and therefore most will need targeted intervention. The third triangle shows that most students in the school are in need of intensive intervention.

Willingness to take a hard look at student achievement is a crucial element in shaping an effective prevention/intervention system. We must put political pressures aside and do what is right for our students. Each district is unique and schools within a district will fall at different ranges within an RtI configuration. Understanding and embracing your pyramid plays an important part in implementation planning, student goals, choice of curriculum, scheduling, personnel, and allocation of funds. We must understand that the tiers of a literacy system are not static but rather serve as a continuum of instruction. This is merely a first step in understanding your current status based on an RtI model. It allows educators to move forward with realistic plans to change their configuration after realistically confronting the challenges that face them. In an effective RtI system, students are moved from tier to tier based on their individual progress. Over time, with effort, your RtI pyramid will change to reflect the optimum configuration in which most students achieve at grade level.

Figure 1.5 *What does your school look like?*

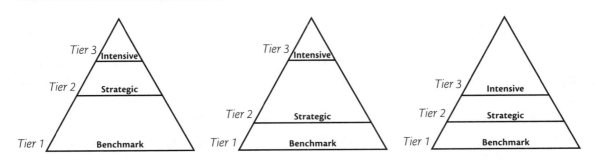

In order to determine student instructional need, Fuchs and Fuchs (2007, p. 16) as well as NASDSE (Batsche, et al., 2007, p. 20) recommend reliable and valid universal screening for all students in the beginning of the school year. They also suggest screening/progress monitoring three times during the year. Batsche, et al., also advises the use of diagnostic assessments to specifically identify areas requiring prevention and/or intervention.

Reading First Support website (www.readingfirstsupport.us) provides information on types of assessments and asserts that the assessment must be valid and reliable and include the five essential skills identified by the National Reading Panel (2000): phonemic awareness, phonics, vocabulary, fluency, and comprehension. Reading First Technical Assistance Centers also provide information about specific assessments. The California Reading First plan, for example, provides a comprehensive description of approved assessments for Reading First Schools(www.cde.ca.gov/nclb/sr/rf/documents/crfex24.pdf). Whether you are a Reading First School or not, the information on these websites can help to identify which assessments can be used to determine your students' areas of difficulty. In addition to the resources cited previously, district/schools may elect to utilize standardized state assessments as a first screening to determine potential placement within tiers and then follow that with a second screening and diagnostics in the five essential skills.

KEYS TO SUCCESS

- Identify which elements or combination thereof will be of use to determine tier placement (e.g., state test, universal screening, grades, teacher recommendation).
- Determine cut points for Tiers 1, 2, and 3.
- Develop a plan for administering, scoring, and analyzing screening data.
- Choose a universal screening that will be administered across a district to enable comparison.
- Consider a screening in phonemic awareness for entering kindergarten students.
- Choose a screening that is easy to administer and score.
- Make sure that the data forms and reports are in a teacher-friendly format for easy analysis and continuity across the district.
- Determine the numbers of students who fall into each tier.
- Identify diagnostics assessments that will be administered to students who fall within Tiers 2 and 3.
- Provide training and practice for all educators who will be administering, scoring, and analyzing data using a standard protocol.

THE WORKSHEETS

The worksheets that follow will help you document student need and determine your district/school's configuration in a tiered instructional system. The worksheets can be used as designed or can serve as a starting point in developing your own documentation. Use Worksheets 1.5a and 1.5b to identify screening and diagnostic assessments, as well as criteria for placement and instructional need. Use Worksheet 1.5c to record the numbers and percentages of students in each grade as well as the student populations that fall into each tier. Use Worksheet 1.5d to develop your own RtI pyramid that depicts the assessed configuration of your school. Use Figure 1.5 as a model.

Worksheet 1.5a *Determining Need (first screening)*

Criteria for literacy intervention: Grades _____ to _____

First screening	Name of assessment	Benchmark criteria (Tier 1)	Strategic criteria (Tier 2)	Intensive criteria (Tier 3)	Administered by	Scores submitted to	Due date
Standardized test							
Universal screening							
Progress monitoring							
Teacher recommendation							
Individual education plan (IEP)							
English proficiency							

Worksheet 1.5b *Determining Need (secondary sources)*

Second screening assessments: Grades _____ to _____

Diagnostic assessments	Name of assessment	Qualifying score benchmark (Tier 1)	Qualifying score strategic (Tier 2)	Qualifying score intensive (Tier 3)	Administered by	Due date
Phonemic Awareness						
Phonics						
Vocabulary						
Fluency						
Comprehension						
Writing sample						

Worksheet 1.5c *Determining Need (quantify number of students)*

Total number of qualifying students in (district/school name) _____

Grade	Benchmark (Tier 1)	Strategic (Tier 2)	Intensive (Tier 3)
K			
1			
2			
3			
4			
5			
6			
Totals and percentages			
General education			
Special education			
ELLs			
Free and reduced lunch			

Worksheet 1.5d
Embrace Your RtI Configuration

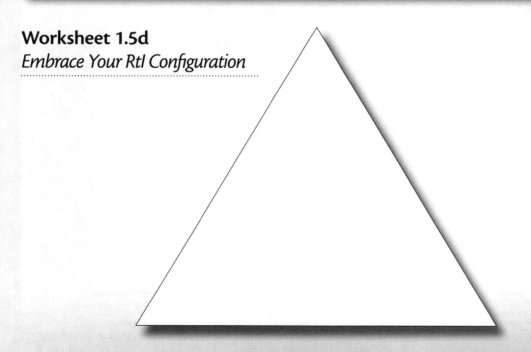

Class Configurations and Schedules

THE CHALLENGE

Once the composition of your RtI pyramid is determined, the next step is to translate that information to the school site. Developing a structure that supports an effective prevention/intervention system is a challenge that many do not want to consider. It requires changes in scheduling, allocation of personnel, instruction and intervention duration, and instructional practice. When discussing the Florida model of Reading First and Response to Intervention, Torgesen (2007, p. 3) stated, "One of the basic lessons we are learning from intervention research, as well as from experience in schools that have been applying the RtI model, is that students should be provided time in interventions that is *proportional to the extent they are behind in reading.*" Realistically, elementary education changes under an RtI model. States and/or districts may develop plans not easily convertible to implementation at individual schools sites. For example, Fuchs and Fuchs (2007) recommend one-on-one instruction for intensive students. However, in schools with large numbers of intensive students, is a one-on-one instructional model feasible? Can students receive the necessary instruction in different configurations and still succeed? Should the K–3 instructional model differ from instruction in grades 4–5? In many cases, without articulated guidance, districts and schools may reach a level of frustration that prevents them from addressing the challenge at all.

THE SOLUTION

Let's start with the agreement that literacy is a—if not the—priority for elementary education. With that agreement, a district and its schools have several decisions to make. It is important to recognize that each school within a district has unique needs, and therefore the configuration of classes may be different from school to school. In some instances, districts provide basic guidelines and the school staff translates them into workable plans at the school site. In other cases, individual schools develop autonomous plans around prevention/intervention to reach student achievement goals. In either case, a series of decisions are made to provide the structure for the instructional changes that will follow. As you make these first decisions, remember that they are not written in stone. The first year of implementation of any innovation equates to year zero. It is during this time that different structural configurations are implemented and evaluated to determine which ones garner the most success and best serve the students.

Logistically, the first step is to create an organizational structure in which any model of RtI can flourish. Scheduling, instructional duration, and class configuration provide the basis for a manageable structure and often present the most significant challenges for tiered instruction. A concern about intervention is that time will be taken from other educational activity. The goal is to make the schedule flexible enough to meet the needs of staff and students while maintaining a degree of structure familiar enough to relieve the anxiety of the stakeholders.

The duration of grade-level instruction in Reading/Language Arts may vary from district to district and school to school. To begin the discussion, let's assume that the school provides 90 minutes of instruction for Language Arts. Some districts and schools add time for differentiation of instruction as well as for academic English-language development for ELLs. Classes are heterogeneously populated, and during differentiation, students move into small groups according to assessed needs. The teacher moves from group to group providing necessary instruction and feedback. The first question to ask is: can the teacher provide sufficient instruction if he/she is attending to several small groups at different achievement levels within a limited time period? Researchers agree that intervention should be administered *beyond* the Reading/Language Arts class. Fuchs and Fuchs (2007), for example, recommend 45 minutes per day for four days per week in small groups for Tier 2 instruction. However, 45 minutes of actual instruction often translates into 60 minutes of class time to allow for housekeeping, homework review, and interruptions. Recognizing the realities of classroom instruction and management can help to organize a system that supports the implementation of RtI. Therefore, districts/schools should first review their current time allocation to determine the optimum duration for literacy instruction and intervention in grades K–3 and 4–5.

> *"It is important to recognize that each school within a district has unique needs, and therefore the configuration of classes may be different from school to school."*

Once the time allocation has been determined, the next step is to manipulate the schedule and class configuration that will allow for various models for implementation. The first years of RtI implementation are an opportunity to develop manageable, high-fidelity plans that can be embraced and executed based on the capacity of the staff and the needs of the students. In a review of implementation research, Fixen and colleagues (2005) discuss the need to implement any evidence-based practice with fidelity before alteration. They reference the Dissemination Working Group's (1999, p. 17) contention that striving for fidelity of program and organization is essential so that if changes or innovations occur in the future we can be sure that they are necessary and not an effort to avoid accountability for the current practice being implemented. Fixen and colleagues (2005, p. 16) assert that, "changes in skill levels, organizational capacity, organizational culture, and so on require education, practice, and time to mature." As knowledge, practice, and expertise are developed, levels of sophistication are added that result in a seamless instructional model of instruction and intervention. Therefore, we must recognize that the RtI process will evolve as the capacity of the staff increases.

When developing a schedule and class configuration, we must remember that what is appropriate for grades K–3 might not be appropriate for grades 4–5. In grades 4–5, we have historical student performance data that allow for earlier identification of students in need of intervention, while implementation in K–3 might demand a more fluid model of instruction and intervention. Consider the following five options:

Option 1

- Additional time is added to the Reading/Language Arts class.
- Reading/Language Arts classes are scheduled throughout the day.
- Students in Tier 1 and Tier 2 are heterogeneously grouped and receive instruction with a research-based core curriculum. Students are then placed in small, flexible groups according to assessed need, and teachers provide targeted instruction for each group.
- Tier 3 students are homogenously grouped and instructed in a research-based intense intervention curriculum that replaces the core curriculum. Tier 3 students have the smallest student/teacher ratios. After Reading/Language Arts time, Tier 3 students return to heterogeneously grouped classes unless otherwise specified by an Individual Education Plan (IEP).

Option 2

- Additional time is added to the Reading/Language Arts class for differentiation and intervention.
- Classes are parallel-scheduled; they occur at the same time of the day.
- Students in Tier 1 and Tier 2 are heterogeneously grouped and receive instruction in a research-based core curriculum.
- During differentiation time, students "walk to read" and actually move to homogeneously grouped classes that target their specific needs. Tier 2 classes have smaller student/teacher ratios and are usually taught in small groups by qualified personnel.
- Tier 3 students are homogeneously grouped and instructed in an intense intervention curriculum that replaces the core curriculum. Tier 3 classes have the smallest student/teacher ratios.
- After Reading/Language Arts and differentiation, Tier 3 students return to heterogeneously grouped classes unless otherwise specified by an IEP.

Option 3

- Additional time is added to the Reading/Language Arts class for enrichment or intervention.
- Classes are parallel-scheduled.
- All students are homogenously grouped by instructional tier and they "walk to read."
- Students in Tier 1 receive instruction in a research-based core curriculum plus additional time for reinforcement and enrichment for advanced and benchmark students.
- Students requiring Tier 2 instruction receive research-based core curriculum with more explicit and intense instruction in the five essential skills and additional time for reinforcement. Pacing adjusts according to student need.
- Tier 3 students are homogenously grouped and receive instruction in a research-based intense

intervention curriculum that replaces the core curriculum. Tier 3 classes have the smallest student/ teacher ratios.

- All students return to heterogeneous classes after Reading/Language Arts unless otherwise specified by an IEP.

Option 4

- Reading/Language Arts classes are parallel-scheduled.
- All students receive instruction in a research-based core curriculum.
- Additional time for intervention is allocated and parallel-scheduled at another time during the day.
- Students requiring Tier 2 instruction are provided with one period (60 minutes) of targeted instruction.
- Students in need of Tier 3 instruction are provided with two periods (120 minutes) of intense, explicit instruction.

Option 5

- Additional time is allocated to the Reading/Language Arts classes.
- Reading/Language Arts classes are parallel-scheduled.
- Students requiring Tier 1 and Tier 2 instruction are heterogeneously grouped.
- Students requiring Tier 3 instruction are homogeneously grouped and receive intense intervention that replaces the core.
- Students in Tier 3 are exposed to the core in one of two ways: either the students receive a scheduled amount of time in the intervention class for exposure to the core, or they join the Tier 1 class as a designated time for Tier 1 instruction.
- Students in Tier 3 return to heterogeneously grouped classes after Reading/Language Arts unless otherwise specified by an IEP.

Each option requires close examination as to its benefits and limitations relative to the uniqueness of each school and its population. For example, in options 1 through 3, students requiring Tier 3 intervention are removed from core instruction so that time in intervention is maximized. This means that while students are enrolled in Tier 3 intervention, the focus will be on advancing their literacy skills to the point where they can access Tier 1 or even Tier 2 instruction in a meaningful way. In the first three options, students in Tier 3 will not be receiving core instruction. Options 4 and 5, on the other hand, either include students in core instruction or allow for exposure to the core. We must consider if exposure or inclusion in the core will actually benefit students in a meaningful way. Options 4 and 5 also demand careful articulation of the meaning and practice of "exposure to the core" so as not to dilute the precious time needed for Tier 3 intervention. Additionally, each option must be analyzed relative to grade level. Different grades might require different class schedules and class configurations.

The district/school may either set firm parameters for Reading/Language Arts configuration, or the district may simply determine the amount of time for each instructional piece and then leave it to the school to decide which configuration works best. Flexible grouping is essential in any prevention/intervention model, and parallel-scheduling allows for ease of grouping and regrouping. In this configuration, Reading/Language Arts classes or interventions are parallel-scheduled as much as possible. This allows for lateral movement of students among tiers, thus reducing the impact of movement on students and instructional personnel. Figure 1.6 provides an illustration of homogenously grouped classes that are parallel-scheduled.

Figure 1.6 *Parallel-Scheduled Homogenously Grouped Classes*

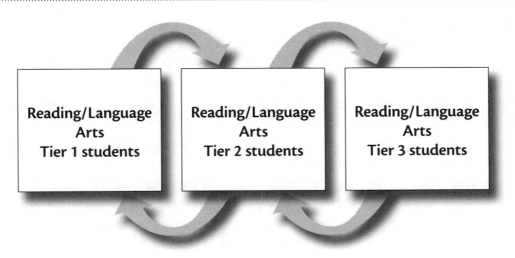

Parallel-scheduling also frees instructional staff so that they are available to assist in Tier 2 and Tier 3 classes for small group and individual instruction. Creating schedules and structures that are efficient and manageable provides the best chance for success as implementation moves forward. Choose the schedule and configuration that provides the most benefit for students and is manageable for teachers and instructional personnel.

Once the schedule and class configuration are determined, the next decision to make is how and when children will enter and exit intervention. Developing a manageable instructional schedule allows schools to employ one or both of the following models of exit and entry for intervention. Two service strategies are discussed in RtI literature. O'Connor (2007) suggests that Tier 2 intervention can be managed in two ways: "by duration (e.g., 10 or 15 weeks of intervention), or by the progress students make in the intervention."

The first model relies on providing instruction for a predetermined amount of time in Tier 2 before students exit, are enrolled in another round of Tier 2, or are referred to Tier 3 based on student response to intervention. In attempting to determine the optimum dosage of Tier 2 intervention in second grade, Vaughn (2003) found that 31% of students caught up to average reading levels within ten weeks, 53% caught up in 20 weeks, and 76% achieved average reading levels in 30 weeks (O'Connor, 2007, p. 144). Schools can adjust treatment in Tier 2 to coincide with school schedules when considering a standard duration of instruction. For example, schools that employ a trimester system might elect to review student progress at the end of each term to determine exit and entry of students. Of course, student progress is still monitored at regular intervals within the instructional time. If this model is applied, articulated entry and exit procedures are essential to accommodate students who achieve higher levels at faster rates in Tier 2 or Tier 3 and for students who may be ready to exit Tier 2 prior to the end of the standard term. If this is the case, the teacher collects the data described in the entry or exit criteria and presents it to the RtI team for further evaluation and possible change in placement. Making change manageable does not mean that we neglect the needs of the students.

The second model calls for the referral of students as soon as they exhibit difficulty in Tier 1. Students then receive Tier 2 instruction, which is discontinued when students demonstrate sufficient progress. This construct necessitates the continual movement of students in and out of Tier 2 instruction as well as Tier 2 classes that can be created and dismantled as needed. We want to address the needs of students as soon as possible, but we also need to avoid a yo-yo effect in which students bounce back and forth between Tier 1 instruction and Tier 1 plus Tier 2 instruction. Therefore, if employing this model, it is imperative to articulate specific exit and entry procedures that include various data points as well as a suitable and realistic schedule for team meetings to determine student placement. In such a system, daily meetings might seem advisable; but are they practical and sustainable? Exit procedures are discussed in Phase 2: Implementation.

Both models have the potential to be effective if carefully planned and executed. However, choosing the ideal configuration for a school initiating RtI depends not only on student need, but also on the readiness and training of the administrative and instructional staff, physical space, budget constraints, numbers of students, and the availability and capacity of support personnel to assist with Tier 2 instruction. At the elementary level, a school may choose to employ both models, with K–3 using a fluid form of referral and grades 4–5 employing a standard duration of treatment.

Students in need of Tier 3 instruction are performing significantly below grade level. Their need is so great that they will require a longer duration of intense intervention. Students are referred to Tier 3 intervention either through universal screening that indicates that their needs cannot be met by enrollment in Tier 2 intervention or if they have not responded to Tier 2 intervention. The identification process is dependent on various factors. For example, kindergarten students have not yet been exposed to Tier 1 or Tier 2 instruction. Unless there are significant data to indicate the need for Tier 2 or Tier 3 intervention, students would be initially enrolled in Tier 1 instruction with alterations to instruction guided by progress-monitoring data. On the other hand, a student in fifth grade who is performing at first-grade level has enough historical data to refer him/her to Tier 3 intervention at the beginning of the school year.

Again, if RtI is viewed as an evolving process, we can alter the structure as student progress is analyzed and/or the school situation changes. While educators grapple to understand and provide a fluid model of instruction and intervention based on assessed student need, we must make the initial change manageable so that all stakeholders can build the capacity necessary to implement and sustain RtI. Consider creating a data-driven RtI process that will evolve as teacher and administrator knowledge increases rather than making initial decisions that become obsolete. A successful model fits the unique composition of the school and community, and attends to the changing needs of the students and staff.

KEYS TO SUCCESS

- Choose a configuration that reflects the reality of student achievement at your school.
- Do your current student-progress data support the class configuration that you currently employ?
- How much actual time and intensity do strategic students receive if differentiation occurs within the core classroom?
- How many groups can one teacher successfully negotiate?
- If you chose homogeneous grouping (Option 3), what student/teacher ratio will be applied for Tiers 1, 2, and 3 classes?
- If you chose options 4 or 5, will students benefit from instruction in Tier 1, and what accommodations and/or modifications are necessary for those students to access grade-level instruction?
- If students in Tier 3 will receive exposure to Tier 1 instruction, what is the method and duration for exposure?
- Are you able to parallel-schedule at least two classes if you have itinerant physical education teachers?
- Are you able to try more than one configuration during the first year and analyze student-teacher response data? Choose the configuration that garners the best results for the next year.

THE WORKSHEETS

Worksheets 1.6a, 1.6b, and 1.6c are designed to help you think about the best configuration for your students and teachers. Worksheet 1.6a provides a form to list the benefits and limitations of each instructional configuration. Worksheet 1.6b focuses on the duration of core and targeted instruction for various populations and whether students will receive instruction in heterogeneous or homogeneous groups or both. Worksheet 1.6c focuses on the structural design of class schedules including student/teacher ratios, numbers of classes, and parallel-scheduling. Working through these challenges will help districts and schools find the right configuration for their RtI model.

Worksheet 1.6a *Benefits and Limitations of Class Configurations*

Grade(s) _____

Options	Benefits	Linitations
Option 1 ■ Time is added to Reading/Language Arts classes for intervention. ■ Reading/Language Arts classes are scheduled throughout the day. ■ All students in Tier 1 and Tier 2 receive instruction in a research-based core curriculum. After core instruction, students are placed in small, flexible groups in the core class according to assessed need, and teachers provide targeted instruction for each group. ■ Students in Tier 3 are grouped homogeneously and receive instruction in a research-based intense intervention curriculum that supplants the core curriculum. Tier 3 students have the smallest student/teacher ratios. ■ After English/Language Arts, students in Tier 3 return to heterogeneously grouped classes unless otherwise specified by an IEP.		
Option 2 ■ Additional time is added to the Reading/Language Arts class for differentiation and intervention. ■ Classes are parallel-scheduled. ■ Students in Tier 1 and Tier 2 are heterogeneously grouped and receive instruction in a research-based core curriculum. ■ During differentiation, students "walk to read" and move to homogeneously grouped classes that target their specific needs. Tier 2 classes have smaller student/teacher ratios and are usually taught in small groups by qualified personnel. ■ Students in Tier 3 are homogenously grouped and instructed in an intense intervention curriculum that supplants the core curriculum. Tier 3 classes have the smallest student/teacher ratios. ■ After Reading/Language Arts, students in Tier 3 return to heterogeneously grouped classes unless otherwise specified by an IEP.		

Worksheet 1.6a *Benefits and Limitations of Class Configurations* (continued)

Grade(s) _____

Options	Benefits	Limitations
Option 3 • Additional time is added to the Reading/Language Arts class for enrichment or intervention. • Classes are parallel-scheduled. • All students are homogenously grouped and "walk to read." • Students in Tier 1 receive instruction in a research-based core curriculum plus additional time for reinforcement and enrichment for advanced and benchmark students. • Students requiring Tier 2 instruction receive research-based core curriculum with more explicit and intense instruction in the five essential skills and additional time for reinforcement and re-teaching. Pacing adjusts according to student need. • Students requiring Tier 3 intervention are homogenously grouped and receive instruction in a research-based intense intervention curriculum that supplants the core curriculum. Tier 3 classes have the smallest student/teacher ratios. • All students return to heterogeneous classes after Reading/Language Arts unless otherwise specified by an IEP.		

Phase 1

Worksheet 1.6a *Benefits and Limitations of Class Configurations* (continued)

Grade(s) _____

Options	Benefits	Linitations
Option 4 • Reading/Language Arts classes are parallel-scheduled. • All students receive instruction in a research-based core curriculum. • Additional time for intervention is allocated and parallel-scheduled at another time during the day. Students requiring Tier 2 instruction are provided with one period (60 minutes) of targeted instruction, and students in need of Tier 3 instruction are provided with two periods (120 minutes) of intense, explicit instruction.		
Option 5 • Additional time is allocated to the Reading/Language Arts classes. • Reading/Language Arts classes are parallel-scheduled. • Students requiring Tier 1 and Tier 2 instruction are grouped heterogeneously. • Students requiring Tier 3 instruction are homogeneously grouped and receive intense intervention that replaces the core. Students in Tier 3 are exposed to the core in one of two ways: either the students receive a scheduled amount of time in the intervention class for exposure to the core, or they join the Tier 1 class as a designated time for Tier 1 instruction. • Students in Tier 3 return to heterogeneously grouped classes after Reading/Language Arts unless otherwise specified by an IEP.		

Worksheet 1.6b *Class Configuration*

Duration of Reading/Language Arts block _____

Student need	Duration of Tier 1 (benchmark) Language Arts instruction	Duration of targeted instruction based on tier placement/ student need	How will this happen? ▪ In core class (heterogeneous) with small group instruction ▪ "Walk to read" (homogeneous) after core instruction ▪ "Walk to read" (homogeneous) for core instruction ▪ Replacement curriculum (intensive)
Advanced (Tier 1)			
Benchmark (Tier 1)			
Strategic (Tier 2)			
Intensive (Tier 3)			
ELLs			

Worksheet 1.6c *Creating Schedules*

Grade levels _____

Item	Tier 1	Tier 2	Tier 3	ELL
Number of students				
Student/teacher ratio				
Duration of instruction				
Number of classes to be scheduled				
Number of teachers needed for instruction				
Number of classes that can be parallel-scheduled to allow for flexible grouping				
Number of common planning periods for teachers to meet and plan				

Phase 1

Section 1.7

Choosing Curricula

THE CHALLENGE

Now that student need has been determined and class configuration discussed, districts and schools have the daunting task of designing and/or purchasing instructional materials that meet the needs of the students in each tier. Publishers have jumped into the intervention arena and claim that their products are the answer to all of our needs. The term "scientifically based" is splashed across the covers of textbooks, often without the instructional integrity to support that claim. In her article, "Whole Language High Jinks: How to Tell When 'Scientifically Based Reading Instruction' Isn't," Louisa Moats (2007, p. 13) writes, "Each [publisher] claims that its approaches and materials square with SBRR [scientifically based reading research], but this is a ruse. And no small number of schools and districts are being fooled." Additionally, teachers are expected to develop instructional materials for intervention students, often without the knowledge necessary to fully address the needs of their students. Consequently, districts/schools spend millions of dollars on materials and development time for instruction that will not work for students, and intervention becomes silent reading, journal writing, and homework completion. It is no wonder that adequate yearly progress goals are not met.

THE SOLUTION

Do your homework and choose carefully. The National Reading Panel (2000) has identified essential components (phonemic awareness, phonics, spelling, fluency, vocabulary, comprehension, and writing) needed to teach the most students to read and write. NASDSE (Batsche, et al., 2007, p. 23) clearly delineates the type of instruction necessary for instruction in each tier of an effective RtI model. Tier 1 instruction requires a scientifically based core instructional program that "has a high probability of bringing the preponderance of students to acceptable levels of proficiency." Tier 2 instruction requires more intense and explicit targeted supplemental instruction, while Tier 3 instruction entails more time and a higher level of intensity delivered with reduced student/teacher ratios. In all tiers, instruction must be explicit. Torgesen (2004, p. 363) describes explicit instruction as, "instruction that does not leave anything to chance and does not make assumptions about skills and knowledge that children will acquire on their own."

Therefore, the primary focus should be on the core instructional program. Without quality Tier 1 instruction, taught as designed, an abnormally high number of students may fall into Tier 2 and even Tier 3. These students, then, are not necessarily struggling to learn to read, they are victims of poor initial instruction. A scientifically based core program must be in place to ensure an authentic RtI system of instruction.

Perhaps the most difficult instruction to develop and administer is the targeted instruction required for Tier 2 students. Students in Tier 2, or strategic instruction, will require additional instruction in at least one of the essential skills outlined by the National Reading Panel. Researchers and practitioners have developed instructional programs that target specific skills in each of the essential components. However, administrators and teachers are often reluctant to review publisher programs and instead develop materials internally. We must ask ourselves some difficult questions about the internal development of instructional materials:

- Do teachers have the content and instructional background to develop the type of research-based instruction and assessment required for Tier 2 intervention?
- Do the teachers have time and motivation to develop the necessary materials and assessments?
- Can materials be generalized across schools and districts to promote continuity?
- Do teacher-developed materials contain valid assessments that can demonstrate progress toward target goals in intervention?
- Are teacher materials submitted to the same scrutiny applied to publisher materials? If not, why not?

This final point is one of the most crucial because it demands the same level of research and instructional integrity in content and methodology for whichever materials are used.

It is interesting that we depend on teachers to create materials without the careful inspection and validation that we require from publisher materials. In addition, we know that most teachers do not possess the background knowledge or expertise in scientifically based reading instruction to adequately develop these materials. Teachers must have the capacity to perform the tasks demanded of them. Are they expected to magically know what to do? Might we use, instead, the same type of "gradual-release model" for teachers that is used for students? Pearson and Gallagher (1983, p. 338) describe the model as a "gradual release of responsibility from teacher to student." Applied to teachers, a district or school adopts carefully reviewed and validated supplemental materials targeted to specific instructional areas of student need. As teachers receive ongoing professional development, acquire expertise in reading instruction, and have ample opportunity to work with systemic, explicit models developed by researchers and publishers, the scaffold is gradually released and teachers begin to develop their own instructional content.

"A scientifically based core program must be in place to ensure an authentic RtI system of instruction."

Intensive, or Tier 3, instruction must be comprehensive, be explicit, and contain all of the essential components mentioned previously. Students in Tier 3 require all of the components in integrated, sequential programs. Dr. Edward Kame'enui (2004) states, "You're going to need a curriculum that's very different in architecture for the kids who are in the bottom 20, 25 percent, because the way they manage information is very different from the kids who can benefit from the core. That kind of curriculum, we refer to as an intervention curriculum because the architecture is very different. The architecture should be more careful in how it thinks about the examples that are used, how it juxtaposes examples, the amount of scaffolding and teacher-wording that's provided, the amount of practice, how much practice is given at any given point in time, how much scaffolding is provided, how much rehearsal, how much fluency is built in." Publishers who keenly support scientifically based reading instruction have developed excellent materials. Again, we must consider the capacity of teachers to develop and administer instruction for intensive students before deciding to dismiss publisher products. That is not to say that teachers will not make a valiant attempt. Are we willing, however, to subject our students to possible trial-and-error instruction rather than review all materials and professional training options open to us?

KEYS TO SUCCESS

- Develop a rubric to evaluate all materials, whether teacher or publisher developed.
- Ask specific questions about how the curriculum addresses specific student need; comprises research-based reading instruction; and includes the correct level of time, intensity, and methodology.
- Know the federal and state criteria for research-based reading instruction including references from Reading First (www.readingfirstsupport.us).
- Consult validated websites such as, What Works Clearing House (www.whatworks.ed.gov), the Florida Center for Reading Research (www.fcrr.org), and state Reading First websites, for examples of scientifically based reading instructional materials.
- Confirm effectiveness data on the use and effectiveness in schools with similar demographics.
- Validate publisher claims with phone calls and/or emails to state consultants and professional references, and plan site visits to schools that are using the curriculum.
- Make sure teacher-developed materials are classroom tested and evaluated before generalizing them to schools or districts, and compare to publisher materials.
- Review professional-development options and requirements for teacher- and publisher-developed materials.
- Investigate the publisher's record on timely delivery.
- Know your district's ordering process; make friends with the purchasing department.

THE WORKSHEET

Use Worksheet 1.7 to review publisher- and teacher-developed materials and to review the types of information needed to make prudent decisions about adopting literacy instructional materials.

Worksheet 1.7 *Publisher Checklist*

Publisher/Teacher _____ Curriculum _____

Contact Information_____

Criteria	Yes	No	N/A	Comments	Reviewers
Age-appropriate					
Meets criteria for scientifically based reading instruction					
Teacher edition contains clear instructions for the teacher for explicit instruction for students					
Student materials contain ample, explicit practice					
Tier 1 (Benchmark Instruction)					
Tier 2 (Strategic Instruction) (identify targeted instruction) • Phonemic awareness • Phonics • Decoding • Fluency • Spelling • Vocabulary • Comprehension • Writing					
Tier 3 (Intensive Instruction) • Comprehensive (all components) • Systematic • Explicit instruction • Intensity of instruction and time					
ELLs					
Gifted and talented					
Includes comprehensive assessment including placement screening, formative and summative					
Meets the assessed need of students					
Multiple levels of entry for Tier 2 and Tier 3 instruction					
Validation					
Meets federal guidelines					
Meets state guidelines					

Phase 1

Worksheet 1.7 *Publisher Checklist* (continued)

Criteria	Yes	No	N/A	Comments	Reviewers
Effectiveness data reviewed					
Meets district guidelines					
Professional references checked					
Instructional validity checked					
Classroom tested					
Training					
Includes research, background knowledge, content, and methodology					
Referrals for quality of training are checked					
Follow-up training is available					
Coaching is available					
Training model includes paths that build internal capacity					
Implementation planning and evaluation are available					
Quality control of training validated					
Implementation					
▪ Articulated implementation plan ▪ Teacher developed materials can be generalized ▪ Provides an administrator guide					
Ordering					
1. Order placed					
2. Board approval received					
3. PO sent to publisher					
4. Order is being tracked					
5. Firm date of delivery					
6. Plans for distribution set					

Professional Development

THE CHALLENGE

Subsequent to adopting or developing instructional materials, it is necessary to organize a professional development plan that will provide initial and ongoing training for all stakeholders. Professional development is an expensive process and is often overlooked, or considered optional, when developing a comprehensive literacy system. Administrators often assume that elementary teachers already have the knowledge and skills to teach reading. Nothing could be farther from the truth. In 2006, The National Council on Teacher Quality examined what prospective elementary teachers were learning about scientifically based reading instruction in their college elementary-education programs. After examining the required courses on reading for 72 programs, the council found that only 11 out of 72 institutions actually taught all components of reading science (Walsh, et al., 2006, p. 4). Consequently, professional development surrounding reading instruction is an area in which we cannot skimp. With poor or inadequate professional development, teachers cannot be expected to change their practice or embrace the science that supports an RtI system. At best, their implementation will be superficial, and eventually one more set of materials will be relegated to the back of the closet. Garmston and Wellman (1999, p. 172) define efficacy as, "knowing that one has the capacity to make a difference and being willing and able do so." They go on to explain, "If individuals or groups feel little efficacy, then blame, withdrawal, and rigidity are likely to follow. But teachers with robust efficacy are likely to expend more energy in their work, persevere longer, set more challenging goals, and continue in the face of failure." With the expense of purchasing and developing materials, and with many students in need, can we afford to withhold adequate professional development for our teachers and other stakeholders?

THE SOLUTION

Clearly, quality professional development is vital when implementing an effective literacy system. Elmore (2004, p. 104) defines professional development as, "the set of knowledge and skill-building activities that raise the capacity of teachers and administrators to respond to external demands and engage in the improvement of practice and performance." Fullan (2001) notes that innovation is multidimensional and we must address three major components of the change: new instructional materials, new teaching methodology, and change in belief systems. As previously stated, teachers may not have the background knowledge necessary to effect change without a significant amount of professional development in scientifically based reading instruction. An expert who has expertise in research, curriculum components, literacy content specific to each tier, social/emotional challenges of children struggling to read, and who has knowledge of the challenges that face teachers implementing an RtI system will be able to initiate changes in belief systems and garner support for this most important of instructional innovations. When designing a professional development plan, consider that teachers must not only gain expertise with instructional materials, but also increase their knowledge of research and the essential elements outlined by the National Reading Panel (National Institute of Child Health and Human Development, 2000)—content knowledge and assessment—if they are to become the diagnostic teachers we expect them to be.

> *"... teachers may not have the background knowledge necessary to effect change without a significant amount of professional development in scientifically based reading instruction."*

KEYS TO SUCCESS

- Ensure that professional development on curriculum materials and instructional methodology is specific to each tier. However, train all teachers in all tiers.
- Encourage all teachers to participate in professional development in scientifically based reading research, diagnostic assessment, and teaching.
- Beware of turn-the-page and free training. Teachers must understand the why as well as the how to deliver systemic instruction and intervention.
- Ensure that consultants/trainers have significant expertise in adopted curriculum materials, reading research, and instructional methodology required for each tier of instruction.
- Train substitute teachers and paraprofessionals, if possible. We need everyone to assist with improving the literacy skills of our students.
- Schedule at least one training after the school year begins for new hires.
- Order training materials early so that teachers have the necessary items to fully participate.
- Designate a member of the District/School-Site Literacy RtI Committee to attend each session to answer district/school-specific questions.
- Specific training sessions should be designed for teachers, administrators, and counselors.
- Plan for ongoing professional development in the form of advanced literacy courses and onsite coaching.

THE WORKSHEET

Use Worksheet 1.8 as a guide when arranging professional development for initial and follow-up training for teachers, administrators, paraeducators, and substitute teachers. Sometimes the logistics of professional development set the tone for implementation.

Worksheet 1.8 *District/School Training Checklist*

Type of training: Initial _____ Follow-up _____ Assessment literacy _____ Behavior management _____

Task	Cost	Funds used	Person responsible	Dates	Notes
Schedule training dates.					
Book trainer(s).					
Book training site(s).					
Design and distribute notification.					
Arrange food.					
Arrange audiovisual equipment.					
Register participants.					
Purchase training materials.					
Set up training room(s).					
Prepare evaluation materials.					
Appoint a school/district facilitator.					

Phase 1

Section 1.9

Accountability

Part A: Mutual Accountability

THE CHALLENGE

Part of any innovation is accountability. We usually think of accountability only in terms of data gathering and student progress. However, that is just one aspect of large-scale change. Marzano, Waters, and McNulty (2005, p. 66) discuss the difference between first-order and second-order change. First-order change is a shift in what is already happening, such as new textbooks. One thing changes but the system remains basically the same. Second-order change is a dramatic departure from the norm, resulting in full-system change. Clearly, Marzano and colleagues would consider district- or schoolwide literacy intervention a second-order change, because it is a significant departure from the norm in elementary schools. District/schoolwide literacy intervention meets specific needs of all children immediately rather than waiting for them to fail, which entails a complete system overhaul. DuFour and colleagues (2004, p. 34) aptly describe a typical classroom scenario that has occurred for years in elementary schools across the nation: "She [the teacher] teaches the unit to the best of her ability and assesses each student's learning at its conclusion. The results make it evident that some students have not mastered the essential outcomes. On the one hand, the teacher would like to take the time to help those students. On the other hand, she feels compelled to move forward in order to cover the course content. If the teacher uses instructional time to assist those who have not learned, the needs of students who have mastered the content are not being met; if the teacher pushes on with new concepts, struggling students are likely to fall further behind." Implementing an RtI system eliminates this situation by changing the way teachers and administrators think about their roles, respond to data, and instruct students. As a result, accountability systems must change as well. The challenge for districts and schools is how to develop both human and numerical accountability systems that provide pressure *and* support for all stakeholders.

THE SOLUTION

Fullan (2001, pp. 91–92) describes the need for both pressure and support to ensure the successful implementation of any innovation: "Successful change projects always include elements of both pressure and support. Pressure without support leads to resistance and alienation; support without pressure leads to drift or waste of resources. Applied to an RtI model, pressure and support focus on mutual accountability at all levels of the system, with support mechanisms that enable the implementer to achieve the goal and hold that person responsible for his/her performance. For example, district personnel cannot expect a site administrator to develop and implement a tiered literacy model without providing training and guidance as well as funding for materials and personnel. However, once those supports are in place, the district personnel must hold the site administrator accountable. Therefore, we must have an internal accountability system in which all levels of personnel are held accountable.

"Educational institutions must develop mutual-accountability systems in which vertical agreements about pressures and supports are discussed and articulated from district administrators to site administrators to teachers."

Educational institutions must develop mutual-accountability systems in which vertical agreements about pressures and supports are discussed and articulated from district administrators to site administrators to teachers. "If resources are provided and excuses are eliminated one by one, persistent good performance is going to be noticed in another light. So are situations where things fail to improve despite new investments" (Fullan, 2006, p. 89).

When developing a mutual-accountability system, it is helpful to use Elmore's (2004) "accountability for capacity" definition as a guideline. Elmore (p. 93) writes, "Accountability must be a reciprocal process. For every increment of performance I demand from you, I have an equal responsibility to provide you with the capacity to meet that expectation. Likewise, for every investment you make in my skill and knowledge, I have a reciprocal responsibility to demonstrate some new increment in performance." Using the assertions of Elmore (2004) and Fullan (2006), the District Literacy RtI Committee must put away their egos and have frank discussions about the pressures that will be applied and the supports that will be necessary to implement an RtI system with fidelity and accountability. An agreement of this type creates a collaborative rather than adversarial environment and fosters coherence and clarity.

KEYS TO SUCCESS

- Ensure that the District Literacy RtI Committee articulates the pressures that will be imposed on site administrators before the discussion about needed support begins.
- Be reasonable about first-year expectations and capacity for support.
- Be willing to admit that this is a second-order change—something we have never done before. Ask questions, seek guidance, and listen to concerns and ideas at each level, because those concerns will help to create an effective system in which the needs of all stakeholders are considered.
- Be specific when articulating pressures and supports. Leave nothing to personal interpretation.

THE WORKSHEETS

Use Worksheet 1.9a.1 as an example of a mutual-accountability document needed at the district and site administrator levels. Use Worksheet 1.9a.2 to develop a mutual-accountability document for your district administrators and site administrators.

Worksheet 1.9a.1 *Mutual Accountability District/School-Site Administrators*

(sample)

"Accountability must be a reciprocal process. For every increment of performance I demand from you, I have an equal responsibility to provide you with the capacity to meet the expectation. Likewise, for every investment you make in my skill and knowledge, I have a reciprocal responsibility to demonstrate some new increment in performance. This is the principle of 'accountability for capacity' … " (Elmore, 2004).

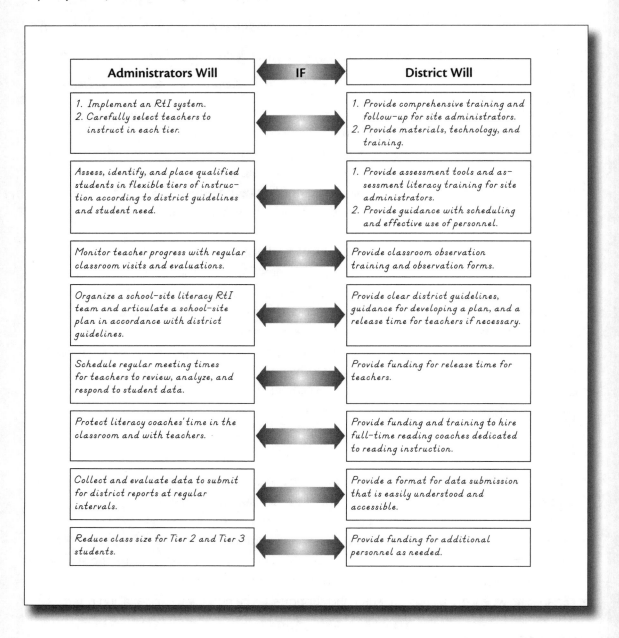

Administrators Will	IF	District Will
1. Implement an RtI system. 2. Carefully select teachers to instruct in each tier.	⟷	1. Provide comprehensive training and follow-up for site administrators. 2. Provide materials, technology, and training.
Assess, identify, and place qualified students in flexible tiers of instruction according to district guidelines and student need.	⟷	1. Provide assessment tools and assessment literacy training for site administrators. 2. Provide guidance with scheduling and effective use of personnel.
Monitor teacher progress with regular classroom visits and evaluations.	⟷	Provide classroom observation training and observation forms.
Organize a school-site literacy RtI team and articulate a school-site plan in accordance with district guidelines.	⟷	Provide clear district guidelines, guidance for developing a plan, and a release time for teachers if necessary.
Schedule regular meeting times for teachers to review, analyze, and respond to student data.	⟷	Provide funding for release time for teachers.
Protect literacy coaches' time in the classroom and with teachers.	⟷	Provide funding and training to hire full-time reading coaches dedicated to reading instruction.
Collect and evaluate data to submit for district reports at regular intervals.	⟷	Provide a format for data submission that is easily understood and accessible.
Reduce class size for Tier 2 and Tier 3 students.	⟷	Provide funding for additional personnel as needed.

Worksheet 1.9a.2 *Mutual Accountability District/School-Site Administrators*

"Accountability must be a reciprocal process. For every increment of performance I demand from you, I have an equal responsibility to provide you with the capacity to meet the expectation. Likewise, for every investment you make in my skill and knowledge, I have a reciprocal responsibility to demonstrate some new increment in performance. This is the principle of 'accountability for capacity' … " (Elmore, 2004).

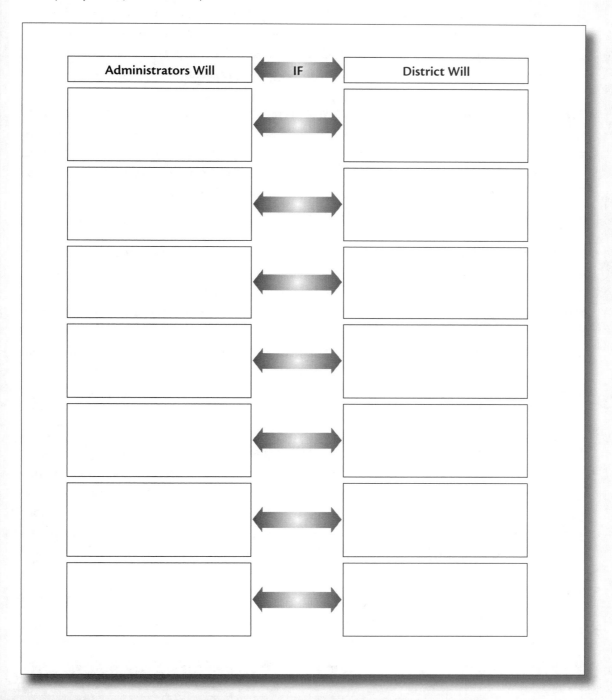

Part B: Monitoring Progress

THE CHALLENGE

A mutual-accountability document codifies the agreements made at all levels relative to the pressures and supports that are necessary for effective literacy instruction. A fluid literacy system requires that we monitor the progress of all stakeholders in the development of and adherence to literacy plans, provide needed support, and meet administrative and instructional expectations.

For district administration: In a district-wide comprehensive RtI plan, the District Literacy RtI Committee sets goals for themselves and must measure progress toward those goals at regular intervals. The committee seems dedicated to literacy reform until the next innovation comes along. Once formal implementation begins and progress is apparent, the attention paid to literacy may be redirected, and the comprehensive literacy reform begins to drift. Redirecting administrative resources and oversight can be the death of an effective literacy system.

For school-site administration: If the RtI system is a district mandate, plans will include mechanisms that hold site administrators accountable for implementation at the school site. If the district's support seems less robust over time, then the site administrator's dedication wanes, resulting in less pressure and support at all levels. Site administrators might also be compelled to implement new innovations before RtI has taken hold.

If RtI is a school-site innovation, then the site administrator leads the School-Site Literacy RtI Committee. The same challenges face the site administration as the district administration. As new improvement projects appear, less attention is paid to the literacy system, and again, implementation begins to drift.

For teachers: An all-inclusive literacy system requires that teachers continually assess the progress of students, adjust instruction to student need, and teach more explicitly and intensively at each tier. Teachers are changing content and methodology as well as targeting intervention instruction to individual students rather than just delivering content according to a pacing calendar. Without adherence to mutual-accountability agreements and accountability measures, teachers become less motivated to continue the difficult work inherent in a comprehensive RtI system.

THE SOLUTION

The aforementioned challenges describe a dangerous but common pattern. Education is currently in desperation mode relative to raising the achievement of students and closing the achievement gap. Consequently, rather than do one or two things well, we tend to do many things poorly. Bender Sebring and Bryk (2000, pp. 441–442) label such schools as "Christmas Tree Schools" and describe them as "well-known showcases because of the variety of programs they boasted. Frequently, however, these programs were uncoordinated and perhaps even philosophically inconsistent." An example of this type of inconsistency occurred at a large urban district during the implementation phase of Tier 3 instruction. Once the implementation had begun, the district adopted the use of graphic organizers for all classes. Tier 3 teachers were then pressured to use not only the graphic organizers that were part of their intervention materials, but also the new graphic organizers, thus diluting the Tier 3 intervention and frustrating the teachers and students. Before initiating a new improvement project, administrators must analyze the potential effects on current programs and decide whether the innovation adds to or detracts from current implementations. New does not necessarily mean better. At this point, it is wise to think back to Section 1.1: *Setting Priorities* and recognize that we will not be able to increase achievement of all students if they are not proficient readers and writers. We must safeguard the implementation of literacy instruction and keep our eyes on the prize: students are literate and able to fully participate in a global society.

> *"Before initiating a new improvement project, administrators must analyze the potential effects on current programs and decide whether the innovation adds to or detracts from current implementations."*

KEYS TO SUCCESS: *District Administration/Site Administration*

- Conduct a yearly review of mutual-accountability agreements at all levels.
- Schedule at least one meeting per quarter/trimester with district/school-site administrators to focus on the progress of students and teachers and adherence to the implementation plan.
- Visit classrooms (unannounced) at least once per quarter/trimester to demonstrate commitment to the plan and to obtain a realistic view of fidelity at school sites.
- Hold teachers and site administrators accountable for teaching the instructional program as designed. Have mechanisms in place for support or corrective action.
- Arrange regular meeting times for teachers to analyze and respond to data and to determine student placement.
- Arrange for yearly meetings of RtI teachers to gather feedback on the progress of implementation at the school site. These meetings are invaluable when revising the district literacy plan.
- Consider conducting a formal external evaluation of the RtI system after the first year of full implementation to determine the strengths and weaknesses of the plan, thus providing additional information when revising/refining the original plan. Such an evaluation should not just analyze instruction. It should include every aspect of the plan, including the adherence to the implementation plan and mutual-accountability agreements.

KEYS TO SUCCESS: *Teachers*

Teachers have two major responsibilities in an RtI system: (1) to teach the adopted curriculum and instructional materials as designed; and (2) to adjust instruction based on student data, moving students within tiers as soon as there is indication that the student is able to negotiate higher level material or demonstrates a need for additional intervention. Fidelity of instruction is crucial in a tiered literacy system. In fact, we cannot measure student progress without first making sure teachers are instructing with fidelity (Biancarosa & Snow, 2004). It is important to note, however, that teachers are only as accountable as their site administrators. Therefore, as we demand accountability for teachers, we must also do so for administrators.

- Meet on a regularly scheduled basis with an agenda that includes data review and planning based on student data.
- Visit other RtI classrooms to learn how other teachers approach instruction and class management.
- Share support needs and concerns with your coaches and administrators.
- Adhere to the mutual-accountability agreements within the implementation plan.
- Teach with fidelity.
- Consider the whole child when considering moving him/her from tier to tier. Social and emotional development should be a factor in placement. Is the student confident and assertive enough to negotiate instruction without or with less support? Would more time prove beneficial both emotionally and academically?

THE WORKSHEET

Use Worksheet 1.9b as a reminder and verification that all stakeholders are adhering to the implementation plan and mutual-accountability agreements. This worksheet can serve as an accountability document as stakeholders work through the implementation phase of the RtI plan. It can also be used as a model from which a specific district/school progress-monitoring document can be created.

Worksheet 1.9b *Progress Monitoring Checklist*

Type of progress	Accomplished	In progress	Additional action required
District Literacy RtI Committee			
1. Attended training			
2. Held awareness sessions			
3. Held classroom visits			
4. Scheduled principal meetings			
5. Reviewed board reports			
6. Scheduled committee meetings			
7. Reviewed district data			
8. Met with teachers to gather information			
9. Refined/revised the plan			
Site Administration			
1. Attended training			
2. Held awareness sessions			
3. Provided classroom observations			
4. Developed a master schedule			
5. Organized School-Site Literacy RtI Committee			
6. Provided site-based training based on teacher need			
7. Scheduled regular meeting times for teachers and coaches			
8. Collected and analyzed ongoing assessment data with teachers			
9. Met with teachers to gather information to refine/revise the implementation plan			
10. Communicated with parents regarding student progress			
Teachers			
1. Attended awareness session			
2. Attended initial and follow-up training			
3. Teaches with fidelity			
4. Observed other RtI classrooms			
5. Attended and participated in site RtI team meetings			
6. Administered assessments and analyzed student data			
7. Worked with coaches and other literacy teachers to refine teaching practice			
8. Adjusted instruction based on data			
9. Collaborated with RtI and special education teachers for movement of students			

Phase 1

Part C: Data Administration, Collection, and Response

THE CHALLENGE

Data are certainly a priority for teachers and administrators. Federal and state accountability systems demand that educators administer assessments and collect student data. In the present educational arena, funds, positions, and school rankings are tied to the progress of students. However, while we have developed systems for collecting data, continually adjusting instruction in response to data is still the missing link for many educators.

An RtI literacy system requires that students are constantly monitored, and a change of instruction occurs as soon as data indicate that a student is in need of intervention. Such a system demands assessment fluidity; data collection; and analysis, not just at six- to eight-week intervals—as is the present practice—but as much as every one to two weeks in Tiers 2 and 3. Teachers and administrators already feel overburdened by numerous state and district tests and may not welcome the idea of additional assessment. Many feel that increased assessment reduces instructional time, which, in turn, impacts student progress.

THE SOLUTION

Reid Lyon (2006) states, "Teachers' decisions should be based on strong evidenced-based knowledge, not beliefs, philosophies, untested assumptions, or anecdotes. Evidence is not the plural of anecdote." Lyon's statement is important for two reasons: (1) it is a declaration that we must move to a system in which student-progress data is the vehicle by which instructional decisions are made; and (2) we must work to change the beliefs of educators that anecdotal information is more important than assessment data.

> " ... we must create a seamless system in which assessment ... is part of the intructional process that guides our instructional decisions."

To accomplish this feat, we must create a seamless system in which assessment is not something we "do to students," but rather is part of the instructional process that guides our instructional decisions. Building such a system will require the input and expertise of all stakeholders in deciding what assessments should be administered, how they are administered, and how the results are analyzed. NASDSE (Batsche, et al., 2007, p. 20) describes the purpose of these assessments within a tiered instructional delivery: "In RtI three types of assessments are used: (1) screening applied to all children to identify those who are not making academic or behavior progress at expected rates; (2) diagnostics to determine what children can and cannot do in important academic and behavioral domains; and (3) progress monitoring to determine if academic or behavioral interventions are producing desired effects." NASDSE (Batsche, et al., pp. 25–26) identifies nine characteristics of assessment used in a multitiered system of instruction. Choose an assessment that:

1. Directly assesses progress toward standards-based skills.

2. Assesses critical components that demonstrate that students are moving toward their target goals.

3. Will show small increments of growth over time.

4. Can be administered efficiently over short periods of time.

5. Can be administered repeatedly with varied forms.

6. Will show data results that are teacher friendly.

7. Can be used to compare results across students.

8. Can be used to monitor individual student growth.

9. Is directly related to the development of instruction in targeted areas of need.

The District/School-Site Literacy RtI Committee can review and select assessments, but it is wise to include all stakeholders to promote ownership of the plan. We must look not only at the research but also at the practicality of implementation with real children in real classrooms.

Another important ingredient in creating a data system is the capacity of teachers to analyze and respond to data. Remember, teachers are new to this process and are experiencing almost a vertical learning curve. Providing training in assessment literacy is crucial to the success of any RtI process. It is not enough for educators to look at barely understood data and declare, "Too bad the students aren't doing well in grammar; I guess we will have to do more practice." Fullan (2001, p. 127) articulates the need for educators to develop "assessment literacy," which he describes as: (1) the capacity to examine student performance and results and make sense of the data; and (2) to develop the capacity to act on this understanding by developing classroom and school improvement plans in order to make the kinds of changes needed to increase student performance. Consequently, districts and schools must not only develop assessment systems that accurately measure incremental reading growth in students and growth toward standards achievement, but also provide professional development in assessment literacy that is both comprehensive and easy to understand.

KEYS TO SUCCESS

- Consult other districts/schools that have developed a literacy system to learn about the assessments and systems they use. Ask questions that include not just the benefits, but also the challenges of those systems.

- Remember that publishers of tests and data-reporting systems are also trying to sell products. Verify any claims and professional references.

- Develop assessment plans that include: what assessments, who assesses, who is being assessed, when they are being assessed, who analyzes the data, when data is analyzed, and what the desired response is to the data analysis (e.g., modified lesson plans or student movement between tiers).

- Include assessment-literacy training relative to the assessment utilized and the data-delivery system. Make sure the person providing assessment-literacy training can help teachers make sense of the data and can explain the expectations for response to data. We need real talk to real teachers. Not everyone is a statistician.

- Remember that data are only useful if everyone can interpret, analyze, and respond to it. If you think you need a Ph.D. to input data or interpret data, data displays, and reports, rethink your choice.

- Consider the time teachers need to administer, collect, input, analyze, and respond to data. Is this time included in the teachers' schedules?
- Be sure that computers are regularly serviced and are available to teachers, if teachers are expected to use computers to record or input data.
- Determine the quality of technical assistance, the ability to add or delete display fields, and the reliability of the server if choosing a computerized data-assessment system. Check references.
- Determine the first point of assessment. Will all students be screened at the beginning of the year? Will kindergarten students be assessed on entry or later in the year?
- Ensure that teachers and administrators have regularly scheduled data-review meetings at the district and site levels.
- Make certain that parents have been informed on how to interpret progress reports if the data are shared with parents.
- Be sure to analyze student-progress data against teacher fidelity. We cannot look at student data without first assessing teacher progress.

THE WORKSHEETS

Worksheets 1.9c.1 and 1.9c.2 are provided to assist districts developing assessment systems to document aspects of their assessment plan. Worksheet 1.9c.1 focuses on the logistical aspects of selection, administration, and collection of assessments and data. Worksheet 1.9c.2 serves as a checklist to ensure that teachers and administrators are supported through this process and, also, held accountable.

Worksheet 1.9c.1 *Data-System Checklist*

Type of assessment	Measurement Tier 1	Measurement Tier 2	Measurement Tier 3	Who administers the assessment?	When is it administered?	Due date for collection	Person responsible for collection	Response action
Placement/screening (outside curriculum to identify students who are not making progress toward desired goals)								
Diagnostic assessment (outside curriculum to determine specific areas of need)								
Progress monitoring (curriculum based or outside curriculum) to determine progress toward instructional and intervention goals								
Summative assessment (curriculum based to determine if students have learned concepts taught)								
State standardized tests (state/local) to determine progress toward grade-level standards								

Phase 1

Worksheet 1.9c.2 *Assessment Literacy Checklist for Literacy Intervention*

(sample)

Task	How to accomplish	Completion date and/or ongoing
Teachers, administrators, and counselors are trained in the administration, scoring, and interpretation of assessments and data-reporting systems.		
The expectations for response to data are clear to administrators and teachers.		
Teachers have dedicated time for assessment administration and data input. Computers for data recording are readily available to teachers.		
Teachers and administrators develop an articulated assessment system plan at each school site and submit it to the District Literacy RtI Committee.		
Pressures and supports for the assessment system are included in the mutual-accountability agreements.		
Teachers and administrators have scheduled monthly meetings to analyze and discuss ongoing student performance data—how it relates to instruction and how it informs the instructional plan and movement of students among tiers.		
Teachers and administrators have access to support personnel to assist with data analysis—how it relates to instruction and how it informs the instructional plan.		
Teachers, administrators, and counselors have access to technical support personnel to assist with technical difficulties in computer-based assessments and reporting systems.		
Teachers and administrators submit quarterly student-performance reports and improvement plans based on student progress-monitoring data.		
Student performance data are shared with staff and parents in a parent-friendly format.		

Implementation

PHASE 2: *Implementation*

The second phase of building an effective literacy system is implementation. Fullan (2001, p. 69) describes implementation as, "the process of putting into practice an idea, program, or set of activities and structures new to the people attempting or expecting to change." The implementation phase occurs over the first two or three years of putting theory into practice. As previously discussed, we can consider the first year to be year zero because everyone will be new to the process and will encounter unforeseen obstacles. This is a natural and beneficial part of acclimation to the RtI process. It informs the planners about necessary revisions and refinement to the original plan as the focus shifts from the ideas of the District/School-Site Literacy RtI Committee to the actual practice of teachers and students. Fullan (2001, p. 92) describes the notion of an "implementation dip": "Things get worse before they get better and clearer as people grapple with the meaning and skills of change. The relational between behavioral and belief change is reciprocal and ongoing, with change in doing or behavior a necessary experience on the way to breakthroughs in meaning and understanding." The inclusion of all stakeholders during the initiation phase can make implementation easier. Dufour and colleagues (2006, p. 25) write, " … achieving agreement about what we are prepared to start doing and the *implementation* of that agreement, is one of the most effective strategies for closing the knowing–doing gap. Those who 'do' develop deeper knowledge, greater self-efficacy, and a strong sense of ownership in results than those who talk about what should be done." While negotiating this phase is meaningful literacy reform, it is essential to recognize that district plans developed during the initiation phase will not look the same at every school. Each school is unique in population,

staff, community, and levels of expertise. For example, one school may have few Tier 2 and Tier 3 students while another school could have a preponderance of Tier 2 or Tier 3 students. Moreover, the knowledge base of one instructional team may be high and require little training while another staff struggles through the initial months and requires extensive professional development and coaching. Therefore, it is imperative that we recognize that progress may occur at different rates in different schools, and resources, while available to all, may be needed at one school more than another.

The implementation phase offers a great opportunity to learn and improve. Remember, school reform is a continuum. Each phase affects and informs the others. As Elmore (2000, p. 25) observes, "Organizations that improve do so because they create and nurture agreement on what is worth achieving, and they set in motion the internal processes by which people progressively learn how to do what they need to do in order to achieve what is worthwhile."

The key word during this phase is "diligence." Pay attention and listen to the implementers. Support them but hold them accountable. Lyon (2006) describes the critical nature of site implementation: "If you find a program isn't doing well, that is to be expected if teachers aren't implementing the program with fidelity. Likewise, you can have the most well-trained teacher, but if the program is ineffective, kids will not learn. One can also have a great teacher and a great program, but if the building leadership is poor and the teachers are not provided enough time to teach and collaborate with one another, then kids will not learn. It is complex, but so is life. The point is when all the elements are in place, students learn—even those from the direst circumstances." The implementation phase, then, is the crucial time when all the elements begin to fall into place. The discussion around continued instructional improvement in literacy intervention reflects reality when we add students to the mix. What occurs during this phase will determine if the RtI process is a passing fad or a sustainable innovation that will help all students succeed.

Awareness: Setting the Stage

THE CHALLENGE

Teachers and site administrators agree that some or many students are in need of assistance to reach their academic potential. However, this does not mean that every teacher will volunteer to teach students in Tiers 2 and 3. This is especially true in upper elementary because teachers at this level do not explicitly teach beginning reading and may not have the background to do so. Once the news of an impending RtI system is out, rumors begin. Teachers may feel threatened by the new approach and will naturally be concerned about the effect on their time and practice. Resistance can begin even before actual implementation takes place. Elmore (2000, p. 29) expresses one of the common resistance mechanisms relative to any innovation: "Educators are fond of responding to any piece of research that demonstrates a promising approach, or any seemingly successful example from practice with a host of reasons why 'it'—whatever 'it' is—would never work in *their* setting. *Their* students are much different from those in the example, *their* communities would never tolerate such practices, *their* union contract contains very different provisions that would never permit such actions, *their* teachers are much too sophisticated (or unsophisticated) to deal with such improvements … "

Without fully understanding the need, components, support, and intrinsic rewards of an RtI system, teachers, administrators, and parents may begin to shut down to the idea of systemic reform around literacy. After all, they have been doing their best to teach students, and now it seems as if that isn't good enough. Educators have seen innovations come and go, and often speak of the swinging pendulum of educational theory and practice. Fullan (2001, p. 81) articulates the stand of many teachers in his statement: "Teachers and others know enough now, if they didn't 20 years ago, not to take change seriously unless the central administrators demonstrate through actions that they should." The media continually blames teachers and parents for the failures of students. It is only natural that teachers take a defensive stand if they do not have the correct information and understand that they will be supported through this tough but necessary process.

THE SOLUTION

Awareness sessions are an essential tool in debunking rumors and reducing teachers' anxiety. They are the first step in garnering support at the school site. Awareness sessions provide an opportunity to focus everyone's attention to the needs of all students. High scores are meaningless if there is even a small group of students whose needs are not addressed. Elementary school, especially K–3, is the perfect arena to ameliorate literacy skills before students develop social/emotional issues that can accompany inadequate progress, causing them to become more resistant to instruction once they reach

Phase 2

middle school. Therefore, an integral part of any awareness session is a realistic view of the data. How are the students really doing? Are the students at benchmark hanging on by their fingernails? How are the needs of advanced students addressed? Based on the data in elementary, how would you predict they will do in middle school?

It is important at this point to be prepared for, and listen to, dissenters. Questions and concerns voiced by critics can offer valuable insight into what others may be thinking and will help the District/School-Site RtI Committee refine the implementation plan if needed. Entertaining various viewpoints does not mean that the plan should be abandoned or changed to the extent that children are not served. It simply provides information that the District/School-Site RtI Committee might not have anticipated in their plan. Anticipate as many questions and concerns as possible and develop a frequently-asked-questions document. Prior to the session, consider developing a method to collect concerns that need to be addressed. This is a whole-school effort, so involve the whole school!

> *"Awareness sessions are an essential tool in debunking rumors and reducing teachers' anxiety. They are the first step in garnering support at the school site."*

KEYS TO SUCCESS

- Remember that the goals of an awareness session are to provide information and relieve anxiety.
- Hold awareness sessions first for site administrators and then for teachers if RtI is a district initiative, because the issues are different.
- Have a member of the District Literacy RtI Committee present at each session to address district concerns, if RtI is a district initiative.
- Hold awareness sessions at the school site so that teachers can learn how RtI will be implemented in their schools.
- Have members of the School-Site Literacy RtI Committee in attendance to present and respond to questions/concerns, if RtI is a school-site initiative.
- Make sure that the stakeholders know that they will be included in the planning process and that the information they gather during the first year of implementation will be crucial to refining the plan.
- Explain the concept of year zero and that the first year is a learning time for everyone.
- Present current district/school data, showing students who would fall into each tier of instruction and how, if RtI is well implemented, we can prevent the failure of many.
- Explain the RtI process; make sure the person presenting has a full understanding of the process and how it would apply to each setting.
- Explain what the process will look like if you are going to implement one tier at a time.
- Use flow charts, tables, and graphs that are easily understood.
- Arrange for teachers and administrators to meet to discuss particular concerns.
- Make arrangements for site visits if a neighboring district or school is implementing an RtI system.
- Prepare a list of professional references and research data that support RtI.
- Present overviews with some examples if strategies and instructional materials have been chosen.

Make sure the person presenting is well versed and has information and supporting research.

- Hold more than one awareness session, and break down the information into pieces if you are dispensing a lot of information. For example, one session might include the process of RtI, the need for it based on site data, and the training and support that will be available, while the next session would include the assessment plan and materials.

- Say that you don't know if you don't know! Add that to the list of items to be addressed by the District/School-Site Literacy RtI Committee with input from teachers and administrators.

- Be clear about the expectations for teachers and administrators. What do you want them to do, and how will you support that?

- Prepare a document of frequently asked questions (which may include answers) with to the following questions teachers may ask:
  - ✦ Will we receive training and support in the RtI process? What does that look like?
  - ✦ Will we receive training and support in instructional materials and strategies? What does that look like?
  - ✦ Will training take place during the school year?
  - ✦ Will we receive training on the assessments, including scoring and responding to the data?
  - ✦ Will we have release time to input, analyze, and respond to data and plan instruction?
  - ✦ Will there be enough materials for all students the first and subsequent years? Does this include consumable materials?
  - ✦ Will we have support at the school site in the form of coaching and follow-up training?
  - ✦ Will the administrators receive training?
  - ✦ How will RtI help students pass standardized grade-level tests?
  - ✦ Will students in Tier 3 be held accountable for grade-level standards? Will teachers?
  - ✦ Will teachers have input as to the design and choice of materials for intervention classes?
  - ✦ Who will teach Tier 2 and Tier 3?
  - ✦ If we spend this much time on reading, what happens to science, social studies, physical education, math, and art?
  - ✦ How will the intervention classes meet IEP goals?
  - ✦ Will teachers be evaluated on student achievement? If I am teaching a Tier 3 intervention class, will I be evaluated the same way as a teacher who teaches benchmark?
  - ✦ How do we grade the intervention classes?
  - ✦ How will students move from tier to tier, at predetermined intervals or when they are ready?
  - ✦ How many students will be in the intervention classes?
  - ✦ Will intervention classes become a dumping ground for students with behavior issues?
  - ✦ Isn't this tracking?
  - ✦ What are the class sizes for Tiers 1, 2, and 3?

THE WORKSHEET

Use Worksheet 2.1 to prepare for each group that will receive an awareness session. This worksheet functions as a checklist for developing an awareness campaign. Add or delete items from the provided checklist as needed.

Worksheet 2.1 *Awareness Session Checklist*

Task	Date	Person responsible	Notes
Develop awareness session content for target groups: administrators, teachers, and parents.			
Compile and prepare current student data in an easy-to-read format.			
Prepare an outline of the plan that is easy to understand.			
Prepare a FAQ document for each target group.			
Identify date, time, and location, and send notifications early.			
Obtain sample materials (instructional and assessment) for review if necessary.			
Identify who will present the whole session or parts of the session. Expertise is important.			
Have a time for small group discussion either after the session or during the session, and collect major concerns/questions to be addressed by the committee.			
Prepare a professional references list including sites that use a literacy system and research references.			
Book audiovisual equipment if needed.			
Order food—make the session comfortable and desirable.			
Arrange for another meeting with interested parties about a month after the awareness session.			
Let everyone know they are valuable to the process and will be heard.			

Section 2.2

The Role of the Site Administrator in Implementation

THE CHALLENGE

Whether the adoption of large-scale literacy reform is a district or school initiative, the actual implementation presents unique challenges for the site administrator. The site administrator is charged with making the implementation run smoothly. This is not an easy task when beginning an improvement project such as RtI. Have instructional materials arrived on time and been dispersed to the appropriate teacher? Are all implementing teachers trained to use instructional materials, strategies, and assessment procedures? What happens when a new teacher is hired after the beginning of the school year or 20 new students arrive at the school office to enroll? In addition to overseeing literacy instruction, the site administrator must ensure that other subjects receive adequate instructional time and that the physical education and cafeteria schedules are set and running smoothly.

As instructional leader, the site administrator is responsible for every aspect of the educational process at the school. The attitude and involvement of the site administrator sets the tone at the school, and teachers reflect that tone in their interaction with students, parents, and each other. Convincing teachers to change the instructional process and perhaps work intensely with struggling readers is a monumental undertaking. The site administrator will ultimately decide, leading by his/her example, whether literacy reform is a priority or merely an afterthought at the school site. As Fullan (2001, p. 78) states, "The principal has always been the gatekeeper of change, often determining the fate of innovations coming from the outside or from teacher initiatives on the inside."

THE SOLUTION

The site administrator can take steps to ensure success at the school site by implementing the RtI process as outlined in the school or district plan, by beginning important conversations around instruction and data, and by supporting the teachers charged with delivering the curriculum. It is just as important to be a good listener as it is to be a good commander. The first year (year zero) of system-wide literacy reform will be bumpy as everyone works his/her way through the process. However, it is the role of the site administrator to stay the course, revise the plan as needed, listen to implementers, and recognize that this is a first step in a long-term process.

"… it is the role of the site administrator to stay the course, revise the [RtI] plan as needed, listen to implementers, and recognize that this is a first step in a long-term process."

If RtI is a district initiative, then it is the responsibility of the site administrator to create a School-Site Literacy RtI Committee that will develop a school plan that adheres to district mandates and recognizes the uniqueness of the school, its teachers, and its students. Schools are not cookie-cutter institutions. Each one is different, and therefore the plan and implementation at one school site will not mirror another. In this case, it falls on the site administrator to bring specific concerns to the District Literacy RtI Committee and to work within the district criteria to create a distinctive literacy system that is efficient and realistic for his/her situation.

If the adoption of an RtI process is a school-based initiative, or the district has left the planning to individual schools, the site administrator is now ready to implement the plan and develop mechanisms for revision and adjustment as the year moves forward.

KEYS TO SUCCESS

- Choose intervention teachers wisely.
- Form a School-Site Literacy RtI Committee and delegate authority, if RtI is a district initiative.
- Work with teachers and coaches to develop a mutual-accountability document at the school site (see Section 2.9a: Mutual Accountability).
- Applaud the efforts of the RtI team. Even a small victory is worth celebrating.
- Nurture the system by listening to teachers' doubts, frustrations, and constructive ideas. However, bring a problem-solving and positive attitude to the table. Teachers will follow your example.
- Keep your word. Do what you say you will, and don't make promises that cannot be kept.
- Observe classrooms formally and informally. Do not let the coach become the pseudo-administrator. A coach's presence on campus does not relieve the responsibility of the site administrator to work with the RtI team and teachers.
- Learn about the instruction materials and strategies. The teachers will be happy to see your interest and will be anxious to teach you.
- Understand not only the assessment schedule but also how decisions are made regarding student progress.
- Work with parents to help them understand the RtI process and its benefits to the students. Don't leave this only to teachers; they have enough on their plate.
- Hold teachers accountable for the mutual-accountability agreements. Provide support when necessary, but don't let instruction drift back to the "old way" or "my way."
- Obtain materials and supplies as needed. Over-ordering at the beginning can eliminate frustration later.
- Be proactive not reactive.
- Report student progress to all staff and parents at regular intervals.
- Attend literacy-committee meetings.
- Schedule literacy classes at the same time of the day. This results in easier movement of students between tiers.
- Pay close attention to teacher skills. Not everyone is a born intervention teacher. Change teacher assignments if necessary for the benefit of students.

- Include teaching intervention in future job descriptions when hiring new teachers. It is important that prospective teachers understand that intervention is an expected part of the teaching assignment.

THE WORKSHEET

Worksheet 2.2 is designed to serve as a checklist for site administrators directing the implementation of a schoolwide literacy system. This is a forever checklist. The obligations of the site administrator do not cease after a year or two. Unless marked by an asterisk, use this checklist as designed, or use it to design one unique to your district/school. The tasks listed can be performed either by the administrator or School-Site Literacy RtI Committee.

Worksheet 2.2 *Site Administrator Checklist*

Task	Date	Person responsible	Notes
*Attended or initiated awareness sessions			
*Attended administrator or teacher training			
*Chose teachers			
*Created School-Site Literacy RtI Committee			
Developed a school-site literacy intervention plan			
*Understood and oversaw the assessment process for RtI			
*Scheduled literacy classes at the same time of the day			
*Scheduled and attended debrief sessions for teachers			
Ordered materials and supplies in a timely manner			
*Observed classrooms (formal and informal)			
Scheduled regular meeting times for RtI teachers			
Organized additional training and support needed for teachers			
*Collected and analyzed ongoing assessment data from teachers			
*Identified and hired a literacy intervention coach			
*Met with School-Site Literacy RtI Committee to review data analysis and adjust instruction			
*Celebrated success on a regular basis			

* Principle must perform tasks..

School-Site Literacy RtI Committee

THE CHALLENGE

The site administrator is the instructional leader at the school site. He/she is also the plant manager; staff manager; budget director; parent liaison; and resident counselor for staff, students, and parents. The implementation of an RtI system falls to the principal to organize, schedule, and select teachers; procure materials; arrange training; monitor progress; and report student achievement. However, literacy instruction is not the site administrator's only charge. He/she is also expected to be conversant on the latest research and legalities for math, science, social studies, special education, English learners, behavior, physical education, art, classroom management, nutrition, and safe schools. Tired yet? Managing all aspects of an educational institution sounds unmanageable, which sometimes proves to be the case. Often, once an initial implementation is in place, the principal's focus shifts to what seems to be more immediate concerns. As a result, the literacy system may become just another bulb on the Christmas tree. It looks pretty but breaks easily. How can a site administrator manage everything and keep a literacy initiative alive and thriving?

THE SOLUTION

Every school has a core of go-to teachers. These are the teachers who not only do their own job but also are willing to help others, organize events, provide extra help for students, and work with parents. RtI is a whole-school process, and these teachers are the perfect members of a School-Site Literacy RtI Committee. Fullan (2003, p. 38) asserts, "We need, instead, leaders at many levels. Part and parcel of the sustainability in organizations is the way in which they constantly spawn leadership and commitment in all quarters by fostering the flourishing of the intelligence, purpose, and passion

"RtI is a whole-school process, and these [go to] teachers are perfect members of a School-Site Literacy RtI Committee."

of all members of the organization." Fullan charges instructional leaders to recognize that other staff can not only help, but also lead an effective system of literacy instruction and thus distribute leadership to those whose experience and passion will assist in the implementation and sustainability of the RtI process. Ownership of a school-reform plan is a necessary action if we want teachers to embrace the RtI system. They are more likely to work through the plan and use the information obtained in the first year of instruction to make the plan better. With the right committee, the site administrator might actually be able to sit down once in a while.

KEYS TO SUCCESS

- Include general-education teachers, special-education teachers, English-language development teachers, reading coaches, educational psychologists, and parents on the committee.
- Be sure to include teachers from K–3 as well as teachers from upper elementary. The plans for each instructional level may be different, or have two teams—one specific to K–3 and one for grades 4–5.
- Include a teacher who can address union issues.
- Provide regularly scheduled meetings for the team.
- Define the duties of the site committee, which may include:
  - ✦ Developing a school-site instructional and assessment plan for each tier.
  - ✦ Attending district meetings and sharing information with the school staff.
  - ✦ Informing the principal about scheduling and movement of students.
  - ✦ Developing placement and exit criteria for each tier.
  - ✦ Assessing and placing students who enroll after the start of the school year.
  - ✦ Training teachers hired after the start of the school year.
  - ✦ Holding parent meetings.
  - ✦ Informing the principal about staff-development needs.
  - ✦ Ordering instructional materials and supplies.
  - ✦ Developing model classrooms so that other teachers may observe.
  - ✦ Supporting teachers.
  - ✦ Compiling data reports.
  - ✦ Organizing celebrations.

THE WORKSHEET

Use Worksheet 2.3 as a guide to develop tasks for the School-Site Literacy RtI Committee. The items listed are those necessary for successful implementation of literacy intervention. Your team may think of additional items that would enhance successful implementation at your school.

Worksheet 2.3 *School-Site Literacy RtI Committee Checklist*

Task	Date	Person responsible	Notes
Administered or oversaw the administration of screening, placement, and progress-monitoring measures			
Assisted with scoring and placement of students			
Compiled data and determined the number of students in need of Tier 2 and Tier 3 instruction at the K–3 and upper elementary levels			
Scheduled literacy-intervention–awareness sessions for the entire staff and parents			
Scheduled or conducted assessment literacy training for intervention teachers			
Informed parents of students identified as needing intervention			
Scheduled behavior-management training for teachers as needed			
Scheduled inclusion/collaboration training for special-education and general-education teachers			
Scheduled monthly meetings for literacy-intervention teachers to discuss student-progress data			
Scheduled follow-up sessions for literacy-intervention teachers			
Developed a plan to disseminate data to school staff and parents			
Compiled orders for instructional materials and classroom supplies			
Developed a library order of high-interest/low-level independent reading books for classrooms			
Met monthly to analyze student data, assisted in adjusting instruction, and determined movement of students between tiers			
Refined the implementation plan as needed			
Arranged celebration assemblies for staff, students, and parents			

Phase 2

Choosing Teachers

THE CHALLENGE

A schoolwide implementation of literacy instruction requires that teachers are well versed, even experts, in research-based reading instruction. However, we cannot always count on university teaching programs to provide that capacity. In 2006, the National Council on Teacher Quality conducted a study to determine the level of SBRR and instruction that prospective teachers are learning in undergraduate courses. In this examination, Walsh, Glaser, and Wilcox (2006, p. 14) determined that few institutions of higher education are adequately preparing teachers with scientifically based reading background and strategies. In their findings, they state, "Given the strength of scientific research in reading instruction, there is genuine cause for concern that only one in seven education schools appears to be teaching elementary candidates the science of reading."

In an RtI system, not only must teachers be prepared to teach high-quality initial reading instruction, but they must also know when and how to intervene. In addition to hiring teachers with expertise or recruiting teachers willing to learn and embrace SBRR, the site administrator must recognize that not all teachers will volunteer to teach students who struggle. These students require more intense, systematic, and targeted instruction than what is provided in the core curriculum. Thus, explicit literacy instruction requires that teachers learn new content and methodology and be comfortable with "on-your-feet" instruction that must be explicit, systematic, and diagnostic. Moreover, children who struggle develop defensive behavior patterns to mask their difficulties with reading. Granzin (2006) describes an emotional withdrawal experienced by many struggling readers: " … you can almost watch children who are struggling begin to turn off and exhibit behaviors that are going to interfere with their learning, beginning to develop a set of defensive postures. Sometimes it looks like, 'I don't care;' sometimes it looks like, 'I am interested in anything but this.' It [resistance] can take a lot of different forms, but nonetheless, you can see kids do whatever they need to do to protect themselves." So the tough question for administrators is: how do you choose teachers that will do the best job for each tier and are willing to build internal capacity to teach reading and diagnose intervention needs?

THE SOLUTION

The best teacher of gifted students is not necessarily the best teacher for intervention students. We must first match teachers to tiers of students for an RtI system to be effective. Tier 1 instruction requires that teachers follow an instructional format and pacing schedule that will teach most children to read. They must be able to adhere to the instructional sequence as designed and differentiate in the classroom.

Tier 2 teachers must be able to effectively multi-task. They will be utilizing multiple strategies and materials that are more systematic than those utilized in Tier 1 instruction. They will also be managing either whole or small groups of students who are not quite achieving in the benchmark range. Instruction in Tier 2 shifts with student need, and teachers must be able to diagnose and respond to that need.

"The best teacher of gifted students is not necessarily the best teacher for intervention students. We must first match teachers to tiers of students for an RtI system to be effective."

Tier 3 teachers work with the most delayed readers. Their instruction will be broken down into the smallest chunks and delivered more intensely and systematically than in either Tier 1 or Tier 2. Again, instruction will adjust based on student need. Students in this group may have developed defensive behaviors, described previously by Dr. Granzin (2006).

The second challenge in choosing teachers is to find those who are willing to learn to teach scientifically based reading intervention. This is sometimes more difficult in the upper elementary grades because the teachers are less familiar with beginning reading instruction and explicit intervention. Teachers may show resistance because they are not confident that they can do the job, or they are not willing or able to work with struggling students.

Therefore, it is imperative to look at a personality match when assigning teachers to tiers of instruction. We can provide professional development for teachers to build their capacity, but we cannot make them work well with every group of students. We must be realistic. For example, some teachers gravitate toward kindergarten, special education, or grade 5 because it is their niche. They are comfortable with a particular group of students and have high expectations for them. We must now find the teachers who fit best, are able to do the job, and have high expectations for students in Tier 1, Tier 2, or Tier 3. Do not be afraid to change the assignment of a teacher who, after time and support, does not fit with the group of students they are currently teaching.

KEYS TO SUCCESS

Choose teachers who:
- Understand the academic, social, and emotional characteristics of the tier of students they will be teaching.
- Believe that all students can, and deserve to, learn to read and write.
- Have high expectations for all students.
- Have the organizational skills necessary for the effective implementation of the assigned tier.
- Demonstrate good classroom-management skills.
- Are organized and able to work in small groups.
- Are able to multitask.
- Are open to new content, research, and instructional methodology.
- Already apply direct-instruction techniques in their classrooms.

Phase 2

- Change instruction based on student progress.
- Are willing to accept coaching.
- Do not stigmatize intervention classes by creating a situation in which "those teachers" teach "those kids."
- Have patience and endurance.

THE WORKSHEET

Worksheet 2.4 provides a structure in which to analyze the personal and instructional qualities of teachers who may be teaching initial literacy instruction and intervention. Use this form as a catalyst for discussion and selection of teachers for each tier of instruction.

Worksheet 2.4 *Choosing Intervention Teachers*

Candidate teacher _____ Date _____

Qualities	Yes/No	Notes
Believes that all children can learn to read and write.		
Has good organizational skills.		
Has good classroom management and behavior management skills.		
Is able to accept coaching.		
Works well with others.		
Has good communication skills.		
Continuously refines teaching practices based on student progress.		
Works well with struggling students.		
Continuously monitors student progress.		
Is willing to try new instructional methodologies.		
Works well with parents.		
Welcomes administrator observation and participation.		

Phase 2

Worksheet 2.4 *Choosing Intervention Teachers* (continued)

Candidate teacher _____   Date _____

Qualities	Yes/No	Notes
Tier 1 Qualities		
▪ Can follow prescribed/designed curriculum materials and pacing.		
▪ Can effectively differentiate in the core classroom.		
▪ Is sensitive to changes in student academic behavior and willing to recommend Tier 2 intervention as needed.		
Tier 2 Qualities		
▪ Works well with students who struggle.		
▪ Is able to utilize varied instructional materials to target student need and differentiate instruction.		
▪ Is able to manage small groups or a whole class, homogeneously grouped for intervention.		
▪ Is sensitive to student academic behavior and will refer students to Tier 1 or Tier 3 as indicated by data.		
Tier 3 Qualities		
▪ Has patience and endurance.		
▪ Is able to work well with the most delayed readers.		
▪ Has high expectations for students that students will reach their academic potential.		
▪ Is able to break instructional components into small manageable pieces.		
▪ Is sensitive to student academic behavior and will move students to Tier 2 as indicated by data and will refer students for more intense instruction as needed.		

Section 2.5

Placement and Schedules

THE CHALLENGE

Because RtI is a relatively new concept, there are varying interpretations as to how students are identified and placed for Tier 2 and Tier 3 instruction. Most researchers agree that universal screening and progress monitoring are necessary to determine student need and track progress. However, some researchers differ on whether universal screening at elementary school is adequate to target students potentially at risk of reading failure or whether using universal screening will overidentify students who might, given the chance, progress adequately with Tier 1 instruction. Fuchs and Fuchs (2007, p. 16) suggest the use of universal screening plus at least five weeks of progress monitoring of response to Tier 1 instruction before identifying students in need of intervention.

Another challenge in placement is whether to make a distinction between primary (K–3) and intermediate (4–5) levels of instruction. Do screening and placement differ for these two groups? How early is too early to identify students at risk? Does class configuration and scheduling, discussed in Phase 1: Initiation, look the same for different groups of students?

THE SOLUTION

First, we must recognize that there is not a definitive answer to some of these questions. Recognize that each district and school has a unique population; work through the process that meets the needs of your students and consider the capabilities of your teachers in the initial phases of implementation. It is wise to approach the situation from the most cautious position and to remember the goal of RtI. We do not want to wait until children fall so far behind that it is difficult to remediate them. When discussing the 40% of students who are not "born readers," Louisa Moats (2007, p. 24) states, "Intervention can help those children, but it needs to occur early, preferably in kindergarten or first grade. The later one starts, the less positive the outcome and the more costly the remediation. If a student hits third grade reading poorly, the chances of remediating him or her are not good. The vast majority of such youngsters will never climb beyond the bottom third of all readers."

Therefore, caution would dictate that we screen all children in elementary school upon entry and develop a schedule of instruction that meets the needs of all students. Frequent progress monitoring

> *"… caution would dictate that we screen all children in elementary school upon entry and develop a schedule of instruction that meets the needs of all students."*

can tell us if a student's instructional program and schedule needs to be revised.

The Reading/Language Arts Framework for California Public Schools defines strategic students as performing one or two standard deviations below the mean according to standardized testing, and defines intensive students as, "seriously at risk indicated by their extremely and chronically low performance on one or more measures" (Kame'enui & Simmons, 2007, pp. 264–265). If we use this definition as an example, we may not need Tier 3 instruction in kindergarten or first grade. However, students in these grades exhibiting difficulty with Tier 1 instruction would be provided additional time for Tier 2 instruction, either in the core classroom or in an additional class designed to meet their specific needs. However, students in grades 3–6 may already have demonstrated extremely and chronically low performance on standardized measures in past years and would benefit from Tier 2 or Tier 3 instruction before waiting for the results of progress monitoring.

If we administer universal screening two or three times a year to identify students who are not making adequate progress, then we must have a protocol in place to determine student instructional need. Bender and Shores (2007, p. 51) have described a problem-solving process, called "DPIE," for students who are not making adequate progress based on universal screening or progress-monitoring assessments. In this process, educators:

- *Define* the problem, which encompasses the use of various information sources as well as diagnostic assessments to determine the depth and specific areas of student need.
- *Plan* an intervention, which includes setting goals and assigning appropriate intervention for the students.
- *Implement* the intervention, which requires that the assigned intervention be implemented with fidelity.
- *Evaluate* the student's progress, which is monitored on a weekly or biweekly basis using either curriculum-based or independent progress-monitoring assessments.

Finally, after a designated amount of time, student progress is evaluated by the RtI team to determine if student placement or instruction should be changed. Developing and articulating a specific procedure for student placement is essential so that all students receive the same consideration during a placement process.

Because the beginning of implementation can be classified as year zero, a school might decide to employ multiple versions (e.g., one that relies on universal screening only or one that relies on universal screening and progress monitoring while gathering information for a final decision in year one). Any placement or referral procedure should include a problem-solving process based on various data sources to determine placement at the beginning of or during the school year.

Finally, be aware of the school population, as well as the realities and complexities or your school's instruction and personnel when considering placement criteria and procedure. Just because the placement procedure looks good on paper does not mean that it will be realized in the classroom setting.

KEYS TO SUCCESS

- Review school achievement results for the past three years before developing class schedules for an RtI model.

- Contact similar elementary schools that have employed an RtI model to discover successful structures and obstacles.
- Provide universal screening and progress monitoring for all students.
- Develop a problem-solving process for placement.
- Parallel-schedule all Reading/Language Arts classes, being sure to include extra time for specialized instruction. If the school employs itinerant physical-education teachers, schedule at least two classes at the same time of the day for lateral movement (see *Figure 1.6* in Section 1.6: Class Configurations and Schedules).
- Provide two hours of instruction for Reading/Language Arts regardless of tier.
- Provide an extra 30 minutes to one hour of instruction for Tiers 1 and 2 prevention intervention, which could include:
  + Enrichment for advanced students (Tier 1) across the curriculum.
  + Reinforcement and enhancement for benchmark (Tier 1) students across the curriculum.
  + English-language development for ELLs.
  + Targeted instruction in literacy skills utilized across the curriculum for strategic (Tier 2) students.
- Ensure that Tier 3 students receive replacement curriculum for Tier 1 and have added time for reinforcement, tutoring, and literacy skills utilized across the curriculum.

THE WORKSHEET

Use Worksheet 2.5 to document the discussion around district/school policy for placement of students in K–3 and grades 4–5. Specifically list the benefits and detriments to each possible decision. Think through all the ramifications of your decision relative to serving the students and the realistic effects on your school configuration.

Worksheet 2.5 *Making Policy Decisions About Placement and Scheduling*

Decision point	Pros	Cons	Notes, concerns, ideas
Kindergarten–Grades 2 or 3			
Universal screening is used to identify Tiers 1, 2, and 3 students.			
Universal screening and first-progress monitoring are used to identify Tiers 1, 2, and 3 students.			
All students are enrolled in Tier 1 instruction and identified as Tiers 2 or 3 after the first progress–monitoring assessment.			
Reading/Language Arts time is scheduled for two hours per day.			
Extra time is added (30–60 minutes) to the Reading/Language Arts block for all students for specific instructional needs.			
Reading/Language Arts is scheduled for the same time of the day.			
Additional time for tier-specific instruction is blocked with Reading/Language Arts.			
Grades 4–6			
Universal screening is used to identify Tiers 1, 2, and 3 students.			
Universal screening and first-progress monitoring are used to identify Tiers 1, 2, and 3 students.			
Reading/Language Arts time is scheduled for two hours per day.			
Extra time is added to the Reading/Language Arts block for all students for specific instructional needs.			
Reading/Language Arts is scheduled for the same time of the day.			
Additional time for tier-specific instruction is blocked with Reading/Language Arts.			

Confirmation of Placement

THE CHALLENGE

Even with careful screening, it is possible to incorrectly place a student in an instructional tier. Once instruction has begun, the teacher may feel that the student is misplaced and either requires more or less intervention. What will the teacher do with this information? Is it enough that the teacher *thinks* that the student is misplaced? What mechanisms are in place to confirm initial placement of students? It bears repeating that, "anecdote is not the plural of evidence" (Lyon, 2006). So, how can we be sure that the student is receiving the instruction they require?

THE SOLUTION

No screening or placement system is infallible. We must develop procedures for all possibilities. Students might have social/emotional issues that affected their performance resulting in placement in an intervention tier, or, conversely, the students might have guessed on placement assessments, when they are actually in need of more intense intervention. The assessments might not have been administered correctly or the student just simply had a bad day. Even with the most thorough process, we must provide a safety net that catches students who are misplaced, not after progress monitoring but as soon as the student demonstrates the need. However, it is not enough for the teacher to decide that a student should be moved, but, rather the teacher with the Literacy RtI Committee must review the data and affective elements that might have caused the student to overperform or underperform on one or more placement measures. We don't want students languishing in a class that is not appropriate for them.

> *"Even with the most thorough process, we must provide a safety net that catches students who are misplaced, not after progress monitoring but as soon as the student demonstrates the need."*

KEYS TO SUCCESS

- Conduct weekly Literacy RtI Committee meetings, in the beginning of the school year, that focus on placement results and teacher feedback on the appropriate placement of students.
- Develop a procedure that requires the teacher to collect data about the student before referring the student to the Literacy RtI Committee.

Phase 2

- Look at the whole child. Include any social/emotional factors that might have influenced placement.
- Bring any available historical data relative to the student's performance into the discussion.
- Determine a monitoring plan for the student regardless of final determination.
- Be sure that the site administrator, teacher, and the School-Site Literacy RtI Committee are all involved in the final placement decision.
- Consider the teacher who will receive the student that is moved from an intervention tier to Tier 1. Will that teacher closely monitor the child to collect further information? Is the new teacher adept at differentiation within the core class?
- Articulate your plan for monitoring the progress of the student.

THE WORKSHEET

Worksheet 2.6 is designed to document assessment and anecdotal data about a student who may be misplaced. Articulate a procedure that will be followed in every instance of suspected student misplacement.

Worksheet 2.6 *Confirmation of Placement Worksheet*

Student name _____ Core (Tier 1) _____ Strategic (Tier 2) _____ Intensive (Tier 3) _____

Evidence	Meets or exceeds criteria for current tier placement	Does not meet criteria for current tier placement	Placement recommendation based on assessment and anecdotal data
Original placement data (universal screening; collected by teacher)			
Formative/ongoing assessment data (collected by teacher)			
Progress-monitoring data (collected by teacher)			
Most recent standardized test data (collected by teacher)			
Grades across the curriculum that support teacher contention that a student is misplaced			
Readministration of screening and placement measures			

Social/emotional/second-language factors that may have affected screening results	
Method of monitoring student performance if placement will or will not change	

Phase 2

Section 2.7

New Students

THE CHALLENGE

Invariably, new students appear on the doorstep of every school after the school year begins. A comprehensive literacy system requires careful allocation of resources that may or may not easily accommodate new students. Class/group size is a critical factor in Tier 2 and Tier 3. Nonetheless, the student may or may not come with records and test scores from previous schools. The entire purpose of an RtI model is to provide appropriate instruction based on student need. Therefore, we cannot just put a new student in any class that has space.

THE SOLUTION

Assuming the school has developed a careful screening and placement procedure, new students can be assessed and placed with or without historical data. If the student is moving within the district, central assessment database information can be useful. However, if the student is from outside the district, screening measures might be the only vehicle to initially place a student pending the acquisition of school records and progress-monitoring assessments.

"… the School-Site Literacy RtI Committee becomes an integral part of the decision-making process by articulating a policy that will be employed every time a new student enrolls."

Once more, the School-Site Literacy RtI Committee becomes an integral part of the decision-making process by articulating a policy that will be employed every time a new student enrolls. It is imperative that the policy states what assessments will be administered, who will administer the assessments, when the assessments will be analyzed, and who will make the final decision as to tier placement.

KEYS TO SUCCESS

- Review historical enrollment data regarding numbers of new students enrolled after the beginning of the school year.
- Allocate resources and classroom/group space based on the average number of students who have historically arrived after the start of the school year.

- Develop the policy as part of the initial implementation plan, not after new students arrive. Be ready.
- Determine if the policy will be different for students who come with records and without records.
- Identify the person(s) who will administer screening assessments. Can assessments be administered prior to enrollment or on the first day of enrollment?
- Identify the person(s) who will analyze the data and place the student; the School-Site Literacy RtI Committee will review the placement decision at the next meeting.
- Place the student in Tier 1 in the absence of previous school records and administer the screening assessments within the first week if the school does not receive notice that a student is enrolling.

THE WORKSHEET

Use Worksheet 2.7 to help develop a process that serves new students as quickly as possible. The worksheet tasks are suggestions; your school may have fewer or more.

Worksheet 2.7 *New Students*

Student name _____ Enrollment date _____ Grade _____

Task	Person(s) responsible	Date	Indications for tier placement	Notes
Review previous school records.				
Administer screening assessment.				
Analyze screening assessment.				
Administer language acquisition assessment for ELLs.				
Administer diagnostic assessments if necessary.				
Describe social/emotional indicators.				
Confirm initial placement pending School-Site Literacy RtI Committee review.				

Exit Criteria

THE CHALLENGE

Once placement criteria for each instructional tier is established, we must turn to developing a policy for exit and movement of students among tiers. The goal is to increase skill in Tiers 2 and 3 so that students will be able to negotiate grade-level material in Tier 1. It would seem easy enough to use placement criteria for each tier to determine when students are able to access learning with decreased levels of scaffolding. However, we do not want to remove students from intervention too quickly anymore than we would place students in intervention if just one piece of data indicated a need for it.

Therefore, the questions that pose a challenge for School-Site Literacy RtI Committees include: Which data should we analyze to determine movement? Are social/emotional factors relevant to the decision? How much consideration will be given to the teacher who will receive the student? Is there a time of the school year in which it is more detrimental to move a student than to keep him or her in the intervention cycle?

THE SOLUTION

Even though our goal is to have as many students as possible performing at grade level, we must be cautious about withdrawing intervention too soon. We must consider all the factors that may affect student achievement.

Many states categorize student performance. For example, West Virginia categorizes student achievement in one of five categories: distinguished, above mastery, partial mastery, approaching mastery, and novice. It would seem simple to move students within tiers as soon as their performance indicates readiness to receive instruction in a less-intensive tier or show ability to master grade-level material. However, it is never that simple. Performance categories only provide a band of achievement. They do not tell us if the student is at the high end or low end of the band. They do not tell us why or how the student's learning has been impacted. Performance categories are the beginning, not the end, of our analysis of student learning.

Fuchs and Fuchs (2007, p. 17) recommend a dual-discrepancy model to determine if a student is responsive or unresponsive to intervention. Dual discrepancy includes final status relative to benchmark criteria for each tier as well as slope of improvement. Their rationale for this model asserts that some students may have begun intervention well below benchmark criteria but have made significant reading progress relative to their initial placement assessment. However, the student may still remain below the criteria to advance to a less-intensive tier. Therefore, according to Fuchs and Fuchs

(2007), we must look at more than one indicator to determine responsiveness to intervention. While I agree with this contention, a dual-discrepancy model relies solely on data and does not consider the whole child. Are social/emotional factors currently affecting, or will they affect, student achievement? Should a review of these factors be part of the exit criteria?

"Even though our goal is to have as many students as possible performing at grade level, we must be cautious about withdrawing intervention too soon."

Movement through the tiers is dependent on many factors. Once a student is initially placed within a tier, the problem-solving process continues to play an important role in deciding if a student is responding to the assigned intervention and can be either exited to the next tier, requires additional time in the assigned tier, or needs more intense intervention. As discussed in Section 1.6: Class Configurations and Schedules, students can be assigned to a tier that provides exit due to responsiveness or duration of treatment. Whichever method is chosen, progress-monitoring data are key factors in making exit decisions. Progress-monitoring data show student progress toward target intervention goals. For example, if the target fluency goal for a student is 100 words per minute and the student has achieved that benchmark, he/she may be considered for exit. On the other hand, if the student is not achieving the target goal but has attended and participated in class, and the designated intervention has been taught with fidelity, the RtI team reviews all pertinent information, including progress-monitoring data and factors outside the classroom that may be affecting performance. At that point, the team determines if a student is in need of more intense intervention or another round of the current intervention.

Student movement is also directly affected by class schedules. Parallel-scheduling of Reading/Language Arts classes and interventions allows for ease of movement of students among tiers. We don't want a student to remain in intervention or be denied additional instruction because the schedule is difficult to negotiate. Parallel-scheduling encourages the notion of "*our* students" rather than "my students." Whether using a duration or response model of intervention, students can be easily transferred to classes that better meet their needs. Parallel-scheduling is one of the most beneficial structural components to ensure a fluid RtI system. It can prevent the frustration of teachers who are unable to provide instruction that is best for students simply because the schedule will not allow a change.

KEYS TO SUCCESS

- Consider responsiveness from both a benchmark and rate-of-growth perspective. The student might not yet have achieved benchmark criteria, but rate of growth will demonstrate that the intervention has been working and should be continued.
- Consider student social/emotional factors when deciding to exit a child from intervention. Can the child handle not only the instruction but also the social/emotional pressures of less-structured learning? Would additional assistance (more time) make a difference for the child's confidence level?

- Target the most effective teachers in Tiers 1 and 2 to receive students so that the students will make easier transitions and receive effective differentiated instruction.
- Consider a cut-off point within the school year after which students are not moved to more advanced tiers. For example, if the school year ends in June, is removing intervention for students in May best for the child? Would the child benefit if he/she began the following year in the new tier?
- Develop, articulate, and codify specific exit criteria for students in all tiers of instruction.
- Identify a monitoring procedure for students who are moving from Tier 3 to Tier 2 and Tier 2 to Tier 1. Designate a point at which the teacher should alert the Literacy RtI Committee for re-evaluation.
- Develop parallel-schedules to ease the movement of students.

THE WORKSHEET

Worksheet 2.8 is designed to assist district/schools develop an exit-criteria and monitoring plan for the intervention tiers. Use this form as a discussion point when developing your school or district's policy.

Worksheet 2.8 *Exit Criteria*

Assessment Benchmarks for Tier Movement

Tier 3 to Tier 2 _____

Tier 2 to Tier 1 _____

Student name _____   Current tier _____

Point of evaluation	Move to Tier 2	Remain in Tier 3	Move to Tier 1	Remain in Tier 2
Ongoing assessment in current tier				
Progress-monitoring assessment in current tier				
Progress toward benchmarks				
Student shows satisfactory growth but has not reached benchmark				
Student confidence level				
Social/emotional factors				

Student placement decision: Remain in current tier _____   Move to tier _____

New Teacher	Rationale for choosing this teacher

Monitoring after tier movement

Assessment	Conducted by	How often	Literacy Intervention Committee alert point
Ongoing assessment			
Progress monitoring			
Social/emotional factors			

School-Site Mutual Accountability

THE CHALLENGE

Although the concept of mutual accountability for district and site administrators has been discussed in Phase 1: Initiation, implementation at the school site raises new pressures and supports that require attention. Clearly, any new implementation is going to have rough spots. Teachers are finding their way through material that is new to them and instructional methodology that they have never before encountered. Our goal is that teachers become diagnosticians in identifying student need and instructionally addressing that need. Not every teacher will volunteer to teach an intervention class. Not all schools have the funding to hire additional personnel to teach intervention to small groups of students. The site administrator is charged with carrying out the mandate of the district and ensuring that the implementation of tiered literacy instruction is successful. Instructional fidelity is key in an RtI model, but often it is the lack of clear policy and infrastructure that provides the biggest obstacle for effective implementation. We don't want thoughtful plans to turn into a telephone game in which each person has interpreted the directive differently. Typical teacher concerns may include:

- Are students carefully placed to create homogenous groups?
- Will the intervention teacher ever get to teach Tier 1?
- Will we receive materials on time?
- Will there be training for new teachers?
- Will there be ongoing training and coaching for teachers?
- Will we have protected instructional time?
- Will there be too many students in a class or too many groups in a class?
- How do we handle entry and exit of students within tiers?
- How do we handle placement and instruction of ELLs?
- Will special-education teachers be able to serve their entire caseload?
- What does a collaborative model of instruction look like?
- Will Tier 2 and Tier 3 students miss instruction in other subjects?
- What about art and music?
- Will teachers have time to meet and plan?
- Does this mean more work for teachers?
- How do teachers analyze and respond to data?
- How do teachers manage small groups? Will they receive training?
- Will teachers need training in class management for intervention tiers?

Phase 2

- Will students with behavior issues be placed in intervention tiers just because of their behavior?
- Who will tell the parents?
- Is there a pacing plan for all tiers?
- Is there a lack of dedicated space for intervention groups? Will I be teaching in a closet?
- Who do we go to if we have a question?
- What is the role of the literacy coach?
- Can substitute teachers be trained to deliver intervention?
- What does differentiation look like in Tier 1?
- Do teachers understand the delivery of explicit instruction at Tiers 1, 2, and 3?

"… developing a mutual-accountability document between teachers, coaches, and administrators can only serve to clarify expectations and articulate supports that will be in place."

THE SOLUTION

Not all concerns can be addressed in the first year. However, developing a mutual-accountability document between teachers, coaches, and administrators can only serve to clarify expectations and articulate supports that will be in place. The document also serves to inform the development of a timeline as you gradually refine the implementation process. Training, while crucial to a literacy system, does not solve all problems. As indicated by the aforementioned typical teacher concerns, the day-to-day logistics of implementation are as important as the instruction itself. Only through collaboration and team thinking can a literacy system thrive and students demonstrate expected progress.

KEYS TO SUCCESS

- Remember that everyone is new to the process. Success will not happen overnight, and anxiety will be high in the beginning.
- Target the most crucial pressures and supports when initially developing a mutual-accountability document. It can be revised as you move forward.
- Articulate the pressures/expectations that will be applied, and give the teachers time to think about what they need as support.
- Collaborate and negotiate to develop the best literacy plan for your school. Each school staff and population is unique and will need a document that suits them.
- Begin with the question: what will help you implement RtI design as designed?
- Include the mutual-accountability agreements in the RtI handbook and share it with all staff members.
- Include a review of the RtI handbook as part of new teacher and substitute teacher orientation.

THE WORKSHEETS

Worksheet 2.9a is an example of a mutual-accountability document. Review it with your staff. Use Worksheet 2.9b to develop mutual-accountability agreements between the principal and the staff.

Worksheet 2.9a *School-Site Mutual Accountability*

(sample)

"Accountability must be a reciprocal process. For every increment of performance I demand from you, I have an equal responsibility to provide you with the capacity to meet the expectation. Likewise, for every investment you make in my skill and knowledge, I have a reciprocal responsibility to demonstrate some new increment in performance. This is the principle of 'accountability for capacity' … " (Elmore, 2000).

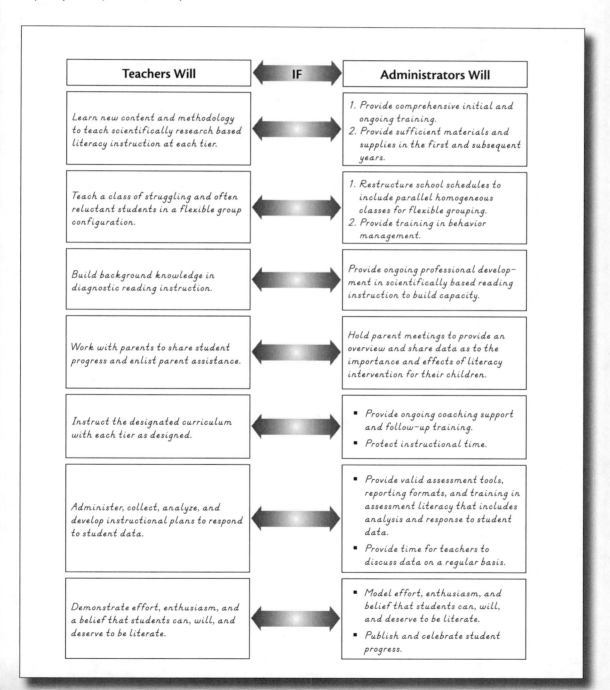

Teachers Will	IF	Administrators Will
Learn new content and methodology to teach scientifically research based literacy instruction at each tier.	⟷	1. Provide comprehensive initial and ongoing training. 2. Provide sufficient materials and supplies in the first and subsequent years.
Teach a class of struggling and often reluctant students in a flexible group configuration.	⟷	1. Restructure school schedules to include parallel homogeneous classes for flexible grouping. 2. Provide training in behavior management.
Build background knowledge in diagnostic reading instruction.	⟷	Provide ongoing professional development in scientifically based reading instruction to build capacity.
Work with parents to share student progress and enlist parent assistance.	⟷	Hold parent meetings to provide an overview and share data as to the importance and effects of literacy intervention for their children.
Instruct the designated curriculum with each tier as designed.	⟷	▪ Provide ongoing coaching support and follow-up training. ▪ Protect instructional time.
Administer, collect, analyze, and develop instructional plans to respond to student data.	⟷	▪ Provide valid assessment tools, reporting formats, and training in assessment literacy that includes analysis and response to student data. ▪ Provide time for teachers to discuss data on a regular basis.
Demonstrate effort, enthusiasm, and a belief that students can, will, and deserve to be literate.	⟷	▪ Model effort, enthusiasm, and belief that students can, will, and deserve to be literate. ▪ Publish and celebrate student progress.

Phase 2

Worksheet 2.9b *School-Site Mutual Accountability*

"Accountability must be a reciprocal process. For every increment of performance I demand from you, I have an equal responsibility to provide you with the capacity to meet the expectation. Likewise, for every investment you make in my skill and knowledge, I have a reciprocal responsibility to demonstrate some new increment in performance. This is the principle of 'accountability for capacity' … " (Elmore, 2000).

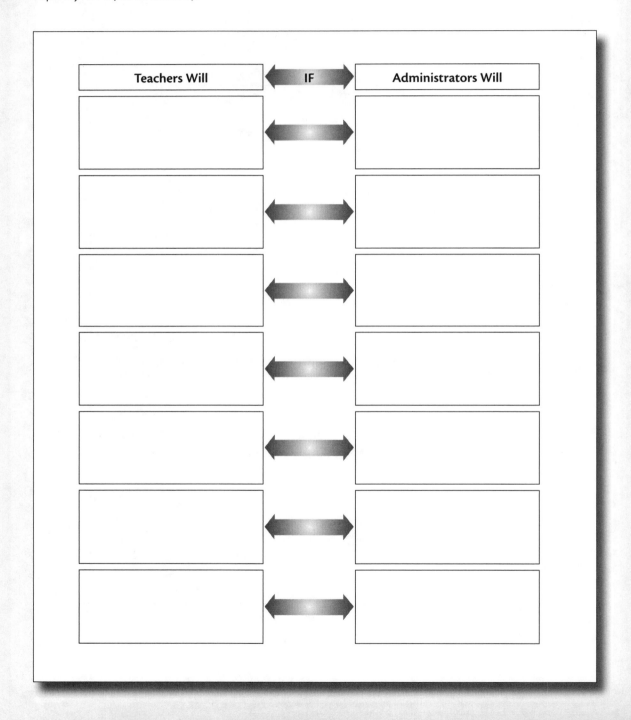

Continuing Professional Development

THE CHALLENGE

Teachers have attended initial training in the RtI model, content strategies, and instructional materials. Implementation has begun. As the year progresses, teachers fall away from instructional practice as designed. The administrator and/or coach notice that literacy instruction looks vastly different from classroom to classroom. Teachers are skipping activities that seem unimportant, and differentiation in Tier 1 has morphed into silent reading, classwork completion, and journal writing. It has now become more difficult to determine if students are in need of Tier 2 and Tier 3 or if the initial instruction in Tier 1 is taught with enough fidelity to reach most students. Student growth, so promising at the beginning of the implementation, drops. Tier 2 and Tier 3 students might not be progressing at the desired rate. What happened? We know that teaching practice is the factor that most influences student achievement. Teachers constitute the heart of reform (Cohen & Hill, 2000).

THE SOLUTION

Even if initial training is excellent, it is not enough to sustain teachers through an instructional year, let alone a full-system reform. Concepts, research, and instructional activities that seemed clear and essential during initial training become foggy and difficult, especially when we add students to the mix. Tier 1 must be instructed with fidelity and at a pace that will address the most students. Included in this pace is differentiation to make sure we keep as many students as possible in Tier 1. We do not want to refer students to Tiers 2 or 3 unless we are certain that they are not responsive to Tier 1 instruction, not because of instructional deficiencies. Similarly, we do not want students to languish in an intervention setting because the instructional strategies and materials are not being taught with enough fidelity to raise student achievement.

Snow-Reiner and Lauer (2005) report five characteristics that are likely to have a positive effect on instruction:

1. Professional development occurs over a considerable amount of time.
2. Professional development is focused on specific content and/or instruction strategies.
3. Professional development includes collective participation of educators through school or grade-level cohorts.
4. Everyone must receive the same content and message so that they understand the range of instruction.
5. Professional development includes active learning rather than solely a lecture model.

Snow-Reiner and Lauer (2005) assert that teacher learning should occur beyond the initial training. Teachers do not know what they don't understand until they have had the opportunity to implement new instruction practice in a real classroom with real students.

Fixen and colleagues (2005, p. 43) state, "The essence of implementation is behavior change. Training by itself seems to be an ineffective approach to implementation." They encourage the use of coaching, progress monitoring, and evaluation as necessary tools to ensure a successful innovation of any research-based practice. Therefore, ongoing professional development and the use of qualified coaches are requirements, not options.

> *"... ongoing professional development and the use of qualified coaches are requirements, not options."*

Discussing professional development for the practice of RtI, Batsche and colleagues (2007, p. 42) state, "Practice and feedback are essential components if skill implementation is expected. Strategies to support the maintenance of new skills are often overlooked in professional development programs." Continued professional development can occur in a variety of ways that include coaching, additional training in research and practice, opportunities to visit successful schools and classrooms, teacher collaboration and sharing of knowledge, and time to reflect and refine their practice with colleagues.

A long-term implementation of effective initial literacy instruction and intervention requires that professional development be provided not only for new teachers but also for veteran teachers. In addition, we must consider all the aspects of an RtI system when developing a professional development plan. Teachers are not only expected to instruct with fidelity and confidence but they are also required to manage small groups, analyze and respond to data, provide diagnostic information for intervention, and possibly teach students who are resistant behaviorally and instructionally. When designing your professional development model, address all the elements that are inherent in an effective literacy model. To build and sustain a successful RtI model, we must build local capacity; but that will take time.

KEYS TO SUCCESS

- Know the background of your teachers. If a teacher possesses a "reading certificate," determine if that educational program was based in scientifically based reading instruction before assuming expertise.
- Use experts in the field (internal and external) for initial training and ongoing training until your school or district personnel have the opportunity to develop their own expertise. What is happening at your district/school site to develop that capacity?
- Provide and/or offer ongoing training in the following areas:
  - ✦ Scientific research on reading
  - ✦ Content, strategies, and teaching methodology
  - ✦ RtI research and models
  - ✦ Assessment literacy—knowing how to interpret and analyze data

- ✦ Adjusting instructional plans based on data analysis
- ✦ Classroom management and procedure
- ✦ Managing small groups
- ✦ Differentiation in the Tier 1 classroom
- ✦ Accommodating each child with an IEP
- ✦ Pacing instruction
- ✦ Social and emotional factors that impede learning
- ✦ Social and emotional characteristics of the struggling reader
- ✦ Delivery of explicit instruction

- Work with your union representatives and district and school administrators to develop a model in which teachers and administrators are *compelled* to attend ongoing training. Attendance at and participation in ongoing professional development is not optional; it is mandatory.

- Hire reading coaches and invest in extensive training for them. The position of "coach" does not make someone an expert.

- Develop a professional development plan for teachers who are new to the system or are hired after the beginning of the school year.

THE WORKSHEET

Use Worksheet 2.10 to develop a school-site professional-development plan. Although teachers are sometimes trained at the district level, crucial continued professional development is the purview of the site administrator and School-Site Literacy RtI Committee. Think of every possible type of assistance that teachers may need when developing the plan. It is better to be overprepared.

Phase 2

Worksheet 2.10 *Continued Professional Development*

Task	Dates	How often	Required attendance (Yes/No)	Content	Desired outcome	Facilitator	Person responsible for arrangements
Initial research and content training							
Follow-up research and content training							
Coach training							
Realizing differentiation in Tier 1							
Managing small groups							
Managing classrooms							
Assessment-literacy training							
Responding to data							
Understanding the social/emotional impediments to learning							
Understanding the social/emotional characteristics of struggling readers							
Accommodating the special education student in the general education class							
Determining the instructional needs of elementary intervention students							
New-teacher training							
Understanding levels of explicit instruction							

Grading in a RtI System

THE CHALLENGE

The focus of awarding grades in recent years has been primarily based on acquisition of grade-level standards. However, students are enrolled in Tier 2 or Tier 3 intervention because they are not meeting grade-level standards and they require assistance. The dilemma that faces many districts, schools, and teachers is whether to award grades based on the content that students should be mastering at grade level or the actual content of the intervention classes. This decision becomes even more difficult if Tier 3 students are receiving instruction in a replacement curriculum. Various opinions will surface as to the equity of grades for children achieving at grade level and those who are not. One perspective claims that students receiving intervention, especially those in a replacement curriculum, are not mastering grade-level concepts, so they should receive grades that reflect that deficiency. Another perspective proposes that students should always be graded on what they are learning, even if the content is below grade level. Political pressures are immense, because the grades received by students receiving intervention could be misinterpreted as achievement of grade-level material. As a consequence, Tier 3 intervention teachers may feel obligated to include grade-level material and then evaluate the students based solely on the basis of achievement toward grade-level standards.

THE SOLUTION

Grading is never an easy task. In an RtI system, with multiple levels of intervention, it can become even more difficult. We want intervention students to recognize the growth they have made and want grades to reflect that growth. However, we do not want to mislead parents or next year's teacher. Furthermore, we must measure students' progress toward grade-level standards. Monitored correctly, each student will have a significant amount of data from which to determine a grade. Consider multiple levels of grading for students, including various forms of report cards. For example, the student in Tier 2 would receive a grade in his/her achievement toward the standards but have an additional grade based on his/her progress in intervention. Students who are receiving Tier 3 intervention in addition to grade-level instruction could get a similar type of report. If students are receiving Tier 3 intervention in place

> *"Monitored correctly, each student will have a significant amount of data from which to determine a grade. Consider multiple levels of grading for students, including various forms of report cards.."*

of grade-level instruction, the school/district must make a decision as to whether to determine the grade based on progress in the intervention curriculum or progress toward grade-level curriculum. It is a difficult decision. However, if the student was removed from grade-level curriculum due to the need for intensive intervention, how can we hold him/her responsible for something he/she was not taught? In this case, as in all grading, the student deserves to see his/her progress on the report card. Imagine how hard it would be for a student who is making good effort and good progress in intervention to receive a report card that does not reflect that progress.

KEYS TO SUCCESS

- Develop a system that reflects not only progress toward benchmarks but also reflects progress in intervention.
- Consider grading Tier 3 students who are in a replacement curriculum based on the objectives of that curriculum. Designate the grade as an intervention grade. Yearly state tests will show progress toward grade level.
- Create clear parent reports. Make sure the reports indicate intervention and grade-level progress if students are enrolled in both classes.
- Celebrate student success in intervention, even if they are not up to grade level yet.

THE WORKSHEET

Worksheet 2.11 is designed to assist District/School-Site Literacy RtI Committees to develop a grading system that will be employed across the school or district. The sample evaluation items may or may not pertain to your school. Use this form to develop your own policy.

Worksheet 2.11 *Progress-Report Checklist*

(sample)

Grade _____ Frequency of monitoring _____

Evaluation items	Evidence	Grading weight	Include on progress report
Curricular assessments ■ *Ongoing assessments* ◆ *Formal* ◆ *Informal* ■ *Summative assessments*			
Diagnostic assessments ■ *Phonemic awareness* ■ *Phonics* ■ *Fluency* ■ *Vocabulary* ■ *Comprehension* ■ *Writing*			
Progress monitoring ■ *Student progress from screening measure* ■ *Student progress toward grade-level standards*			
Classwork ■ *Completed assignments* ■ *Selected graded assignments* ■ *Group or individual projects*			
Homework ■ *Completed homework* ■ *Selected graded homework assignments*			
Nongraded evaluation ■ *Participation* ■ *Citizenship* ■ *Attendance* ■ *Student self-evaluation*			

Phase 2

Continuance

PHASE 3: *Continuance*

Perhaps the most difficult phase of developing a comprehensive literacy system is continuance. Fullan (2001) identifies continuation as the phase in which an innovation or improvement project becomes institutionalized. The infrastructures, policies, and mutual-accountability agreements developed in the initiation and implementation phases help to determine whether system-wide literacy instruction is sustained or abandoned after one or more years. This is not to say that plans and policy do not change over time—they will and should change as the process evolves. However, we cannot expect to sustain an RtI system if plans made during the first two phases were superficial and lacked accountability measures. As discussed in the Introduction, districts and schools often adopt instructional materials and strategies only to determine after a few years that the materials and instruction don't work. Consequently, they look for the latest, greatest quick fix for literacy problems of all students. Millions of educational dollars are wasted as districts and schools abandon one set of materials for another without ever looking at the plan. Countless interviews and conversations with teachers and administrators have convinced me that the term "not working" usually refers to the lack of a cohesive plan rather than faulty materials and strategies.

Continuance is the ongoing path of refinement and revision of existing plans. The initiation and implementation phase teaches us where we need to tighten and loosen the implementation as it moves forward. Fullan (2006, p. 37) argues for the right blend of looseness and tightness relative to implementation and accountability if we are to motivate people to continue a change project. Ensuring that all stakeholders are involved throughout the process, are given time to build collaborative teams around student learning,

and are accountable for mutual-accountability agreements will help ensure that the literacy effort will not only move forward, but will also become a long-lasting, integral part of the educational process. An efficient RtI system will not only serve all students, but will also become the foundation of elementary education, thus withstanding the change in personnel, funding, and demographics.

Creating a Culture of Literacy

THE CHALLENGE

An RtI system will not become institutionalized if it is confined to Reading/Language Arts. Fullan (2006, p. 46) identifies three basics that must be addressed to turn a school around: "The three basics are literacy, numeracy, and well-being of students (sometimes called emotional intelligence, character education, safe schools). These are the three legs of the improvement stool." Beyond these, an RtI system must include all content areas. Literacy is a logical place to start, because the ability to read and write is the basis for all student learning. However, we cannot stop there. In order to stretch the notion of intervening with students before they fail, schools must develop a culture of literacy that pervades every aspect of the educational day.

THE SOLUTION

Awareness, while critical in the beginning stages, is not enough to sustain an effective literacy system. Each time new staff is hired, with every new school year and revised policy, school staff must be included, informed, nurtured, trained, and held accountable. Gladwell (2000, p. 173) writes, "If you want … to bring about fundamental change in people's beliefs and behavior, and a change that would persist as an example to others, you need to create a community around them, where these new beliefs could be practiced, expressed, and nurtured." Expanding an RtI system to include all content areas, and nurturing a culture of literacy, serves to build that community. It is only during the later stages of implementation and during continuation that we begin to notice that strategies employed in Reading/Language Arts have filtered into all content classes. It is at this crucial point that an RtI literacy system can become an RtI educational system. Lein, Johnson, and Ragland (1997) identified seven characteristics of successful schools in Texas that can provide guidance as we build a culture of literacy:

> "Awareness … is not enough to sustain an effective literacy system. Each time new staff is hired, with every new school year and revised policy, school staff must be included, informed, nurtured, trained, and held accountable."

1. The schools maintained a strong focus on ensuring the academic success of each student. The schools established clear, measurable goals that focused on student achievement.

Phase 3

2. The schools exhibited a "no-excuses" attitude toward student achievement. Educators believed they could succeed with any student.

3. The schools were willing to experiment with new instructional strategies to ensure student success.

4. The schools involved everyone, including staff, students, and parents, who could help students attain their goals.

5. The schools created an environment in which students, teachers, parents, support staff, and administrators functioned more as a family that focused on improving student achievement.

6. The schools exhibited an open, honest, and trusting approach to collaboration among school personnel.

7. The schools possessed a passion for continuous improvement, professional growth, and learning. The school staff members pushed themselves to refine their practices, and they celebrated their successes. The themes articulated by Lein, Johnson, and Ragland (1997) embody the tenets of continuance in an RtI system.

KEYS TO SUCCESS

- Do not assume that a literacy system will take care of itself. Be vigilant, and nurture the community around improved literacy.
- Begin to use literacy strategies in other subjects as they apply to each content area.
- Regularly share and celebrate student success at staff and parent meetings.
- Include RtI instruction as a requirement for employment of new teachers and support staff.
- Allow teachers to visit each other's classes or other schools to refine practice.
- Create a research reading group for teachers and staff.
- Ensure that funds for personnel, classes, training, and materials are the first items included in the budget, not the last.
- Ensure that administrators continue to receive training for RtI and planning.
- Continue to provide coaching and ongoing training for teachers and support staff.
- Expand RtI meetings to include student performance in all content areas.
- Create a yearly awards ceremony for students. The ceremony should include awards for progress in all subjects as well as for progress in Tiers 2 and 3 interventions.
- Encourage students to record and analyze their own data and to develop plans for personal improvement.

THE WORKSHEET

Use Worksheet 3.1 to outline ways to create a culture of literacy at your school. This document is not all encompassing but merely suggests beginning the discussion to develop a plan that fits your school and community.

Worksheet 3.1 *Literacy Intervention Continuance Checklist*

Task	Person(s) responsible	Dates or ongoing	Funding source	Notes/comments
Literacy RtI Committee meetings ■ Agenda ■ Notification ■ Attendees				
Identification of literacy strategies for all content areas ■ Science ■ Social Studies ■ Math				
Literacy training across content				
Classroom observations by teachers				
Follow-up training ■ Teachers ■ Coaches ■ Administrators				
Coaching				
Presentation of data at general staff meetings				
Celebration of student achievement including intervention groups				
Development of progress reports incorporating progress toward standards and progress toward intervention goals				

Phase 3

Section 3.2

The Role of the Administrator in Continuance

THE CHALLENGE

Administrators at all levels are an integral part of the initiation and implementation of an RtI system. The importance of the administrator's role does not diminish as literacy instruction enters the continuation phase. In fact, the continuation phase might be considered the most important time for administration. In the initiation and implementation phases, the energy of teachers, coaches, and support staff can carry an innovation forward. However, as time passes, it is up to administrators to keep literacy instruction and intervention alive. As new mandates and innovations present themselves, it is only human to shift one's attention. After all, literacy instruction has been around for a while and can take care of itself. However, once administration's attention is diverted from the primary goal of a sustained RtI system, it is not unusual to see drift in instruction and accountability. Instructional staff will ultimately take their cues for what is important from their leaders.

THE SOLUTION

Administrators at all levels must continue to model what they want replicated. Dufour and colleagues (2006, p. 21) state, "Example is still the most powerful teacher." This must be the administrator's mantra as literacy instruction moves toward the continuation phase. The creation of District/School-Site Literacy RtI Committees help to sustain RtI, but district and school administrators must be cautious in this stage. Personnel who populate the committees should not become the resident experts on everything. The phrase "other duties as assigned" should not apply to them. If personnel leave the school or district, do not leave the position empty. Find a person who will not only fill the position and embrace scientifically based reading instruction but who will also understand and support the evolution of the RtI system. These educators will genuinely sustain this improvement. The task for administration is not to turn away from the RtI system once it is implemented. If it becomes institutionalized, it will—and should—become the instructional foundation at all elementary schools if our goal is to provide quality instruction for all students.

> "Find a person who will not only fill the position and embrace scientifically based reading instruction but who will also understand and support the evolution of the RtI system."

KEYS TO SUCCESS

- Keep the District/School-Site Literacy RtI Committee intact and active.
- Replace personnel with quality candidates.
- Understand that initial student progress will not continue without support.
- Continue to visit classrooms, evaluate instruction, analyze data, and celebrate student success.
- Do not siphon resources from RtI for new improvement projects. Adopt the attitude that a successful RtI system is not negotiable.
- Continue to build a culture of literacy at the school site.
- Refine and revise district and school RtI plans as you gather information that furthers better instructional practice. Articulate new procedures and policies in the literacy manual, and review it with all staff each year.
- Continue to provide professional development for new and veteran teachers to build capacity.
- Analyze the effect of any new innovation on the RtI system. If it conflicts, don't adopt it.

THE WORKSHEET

Worksheet 3.2 provides a format for documenting items necessary to sustain literacy instruction at the school site. Continued use of this worksheet, or one specifically developed for your district, will serve as a reminder and record for continuation of a successful literacy system.

Worksheet 3.2 *Administrator Checklist*

Task	Person responsible	Evidence	Dates
District Literacy RtI Committee			
1. Consign funding.			
2. Schedule ongoing administrator training.			
3. Schedule school-site visits for observation.			
4. Perform yearly data review with administrators.			
5. Perform yearly review and approval of school-site plans.			
6. Perform yearly review of district literacy plan.			
7. Review student-progress data.			
8. Perform yearly review of teacher progress.			
9. Perform yearly board report on student progress.			
10. Schedule performance-plan meetings with administrators.			
11. Order/reorder materials.			
12. Schedule ongoing teacher training.			
School-Site Administrator			
1. Schedule classroom visits and evaluation.			
2. Update and submit school-site plan based on student data and teacher feedback.			
3. Perform continued student data analysis.			
4. Select literacy intervention coaches.			
5. Present student progress report to the district, staff, and parents.			
6. Evaluate teacher progress.			
7. Arrange performance-plan meetings with teachers.			
8. Submit materials orders to the district committee.			
9. Schedule ongoing professional development for teachers.			
10. Celebrate student and teacher success.			

Parent Involvement

THE CHALLENGE

Parents are an important part of any school community. They play an especially important role at the beginning of a child's educational development. If RtI is a new improvement project at your school, struggling students may have avoided detection, or they may have been moved ahead without essential reading skills. Parents may be aware of low test scores and grades, but often this is attributed to lack of motivation and class disruption. Children in elementary school do not decide they don't want to learn to read. Something happens during the instructional process that impedes their learning. It is normal for parents to feel worried and afraid for their child; they want the best for him/her. The challenge for teachers and administrators is how to engage parents in the RtI model and present it as a positive process that will help all children.

THE SOLUTION

Parents are a crucial part of a literacy system. The participation of all stakeholders is imperative if the school truly wants to develop a culture of literacy. Teachers and administrators need parents more than ever as implementation moves toward continuance. They can help their own child as well as other parents and children to understand that difficulty with reading is not shameful—some children just need more assistance than others. Fullan (2003, p. 44) states, "By contrast, professional learning communities not only build confidence and competence but they also make teachers and principals realize they can't go the distance alone. To these educators, inevitably, I would say, 'Begin to reach out to and become more responsive to parent involvement and community development.'" Fullan's statement supports the previously discussed contention of Lein, Johnson, and Ragland (1997) that successful schools create an environment in which all stakeholders function more as a family that focuses on improving student achievement. Mobilize your parent community; let them help you close the achievement gap.

> "The participation of all stakeholders is imperative if the school truly wants to develop a culture of literacy. Teachers and administrators need parents more than ever as implementation moves toward continuance."

Phase 3

KEYS TO SUCCESS

- Include parent groups from the outset. Hold multiple awareness sessions focused on the concerns and interests of parents. Translators must be present if parents do not speak English.
- Send letters and information brochures in multiple languages for all parents. Some will not attend the awareness sessions.
- Let parents help you create a parent handbook with articulated policies and procedures that inform parents about every step in the RtI process. Use parent questions as a guideline for the development of the handbook.
- Develop a parent newsletter that will keep parents informed about literacy events and changes at the school site.
- Organize student-led parent conferences during which students explain the content of their class and their progress in reading.
- Hold regular celebrations so that parents can share in their child's achievement.
- Develop parent-friendly progress reports that inform parents, not only of student's progress toward standards, but also their progress in intervention.
- Solicit volunteers for assistance in the classroom.
- Provide training for parents in the RtI process and include resources that they can use at home. Include demonstrations of each tier of instruction.
- Consider holding parent literacy classes. Parents who struggle to read cannot help their children at home.
- Invite parents to observe classrooms so they can see their child at work.
- Invite a parent representative from each tier of instruction to participate in the School-Site Literacy RtI Committee.

THE WORKSHEET

Worksheet 3.3 suggests types of parent outreach and inclusion. This worksheet provides a guideline from which schools and districts can develop a parent-involvement process unique to their district, school, and community.

Worksheet 3.3 *Parent/Guardian Involvement*

Task	Date completed or ongoing	Person responsible	Notes
Awareness sessions are held for parents at regular intervals and various times.			
Questions from awareness sessions are recorded and used to develop a parent* RtI handbook.			
A parent handbook is developed and distributed.			
Parents are notified that their children will be enrolled in literacy intervention.			
Parents are selected to participate in the School-Site Literacy RtI Committee.			
Parents are invited to visit intervention classrooms during instruction.			
Parents are instructed in the RtI process and how it will be implemented at the school site.			
Parents are instructed in strategies that can be used at home to assist students.			
Parent-friendly progress reports are developed.			
Parent meetings include instruction of the interpretation of literacy-intervention progress reports.			
Ask parents to help develop a literacy newsletter.			
Ask parents to share changes in student-reading behavior at home to be included in a literacy newsletter.			
Parent groups are asked to raise funds for in-class libraries and supplies.			
Hold regularly scheduled literacy celebrations that include students, teachers, administrators, parents, guardians, and families.			

* "Parent" describes parent or guardian.

Phase 3

The Role of Consultants

THE CHALLENGE

Designing and implementing an effective RtI model requires considerable expertise in several critical areas. Districts and schools must interpret the research, and districts must develop plans to initiate, implement, and sustain an effective RtI system. However, this process is a complete paradigm shift for educational institutions. Marzano, Waters, and McNulty (2005, p. 67) cite the difficulty of second-order change: "The common human response is to address virtually all problems as though they were first-order change issues. It makes sense that we would tend to approach new problems from the perspective of our experiences—as issues that can be solved using our previous repertoire of solutions." As time passes, what seemed like a solid implementation may drift, as personnel changes, funding shifts, and teachers go back to a more comfortable educational process. Implementing and sustaining an RtI system is hard work that initially requires more expertise than is available at the district or school site.

Even though a district/school is filled with learned people, their expertise might not include instruction and planning for an RtI system. Consultants—even reading consultants—may have expertise in reading instruction/intervention but may have no experience in designing a viable, systemic plan for its implementation. So, how does a district and/or school monitor the planning process while building internal capacity?

THE SOLUTION

Be realistic about the challenges of implementing a comprehensive literacy system. Be honest about what you don't know. District and school personnel are just learning what it means to completely overhaul an educational system. It is interesting that in our personal lives, if the plumbing is broken, we call the plumber. However, in education, we deny what we don't know and assume we can figure it out.

In *Teaching All Students to Read: Practices from Reading First Schools with Strong Intervention Outcomes*, Crawford and Torgesen (2007, p. 4) cite the use of a combination of personnel to deliver professional development. The ultimate goal of the district/school is to build internal capacity relative to current research and to practice RtI. However, that capacity does not magically appear. It

"The expertise of district/school personnel in addition to the services of experienced consultants can provide a smoother transition from the status quo to a working RtI system."

takes time, training, and effort. The expertise of district/school personnel in addition to the services of experienced consultants can provide a smoother transition from the status quo to a working RtI system. The consultant(s) can offer expertise where none yet exists. Consultants can also assist in research interpretation; specific plan development unique to each district and school site; and professional development in the areas of instruction, instructional materials, data gathering, progress monitoring, and analysis. It may initially take a large investment in consulting services, but as internal capacity increases, the need for consultants declines.

KEYS TO SUCCESS

- Assess the expertise of district and school personnel while in the initiation phase of an RtI system. Remember, having a reading credential or degree does not necessarily mean the program was based on scientifically based reading instruction or intervention.
- Identify consultants with expertise in the following areas:
  + RtI research and how it applies to your district/school demographics, community, and educational infrastructure.
  + Development of specific plans for districts and schools. Remember that the plan must be unique to the district and/or school. A generic plan won't work for everyone.
  + Recognition of the district/school's limitations, both funding and personnel.
  + Facilitation of the development of policies and procedures for an implementation handbook.
  + Collaboration with all levels of administration.
  + Scientifically based reading instruction for K–3 and grades 4–6.
  + Follow-up instruction for administrators, teachers, and coaches.
  + Assessment identification and analysis of assessments.
  + Teacher and administrator coaching.
  + Plan revision and refinement based on data and teacher feedback.
  + Development of a handbook for parents.
- Choose school and/or district personnel to shadow or work with consultants with the ultimate goal of creating internal capacity. Don't leave it all to the consultant.
- Identify key personnel who will ultimately become your RtI experts, and invest in their ongoing professional development.

THE WORKSHEET

Use Worksheet 3.4 to determine areas of need for district and school personnel to initiate, implement, and sustain a comprehensive literacy system. Some general needs are outlined. Use this worksheet as a starting point to develop a similar document for your district/school's specific needs.

Phase 3

Worksheet 3.4 *The Role of Consultants*

Need	Possible consultants (internal and external)	Availability	Cost	Notes
Facilitate initial plans for comprehensive literacy instruction and how it will work at your school site/district.				
Facilitate the development and review of policies and procedures specific to individual districts and schools.				
Assist in identifying instructional strategies and materials.				
Assist in identifying assessment instruments, protocols, analysis, and response.				
Provide professional development for teachers and support staff in initial and follow-up literacy instruction in Tiers 1, 2, and 3.				
Provide initial and follow-up professional development for administrators in RtI and literacy instruction.				
Provide coaching for teachers, site administrators, and district administrators.				

Articulating the Plan: Creating the Handbook

THE CHALLENGE

Strategic planning is a mainstay of the educational process. Unfortunately, those plans are often misinterpreted or disregarded over time. New policies are usually distributed in a series of memos that ultimately become scratch paper and no one can remember the content or direction. In other instances, those plans are so bulky that they are relegated to a shelf, never to see the light of day. This results in continually reiterating what was previously said as we try to get everyone on the same page.

However, systemic reform around literacy instruction requires tight coherence across a district and/or school. The transience of students and teachers requires that districts and schools develop a vehicle by which all stakeholders are continually informed and held accountable for the tenets of the RtI plan. We must all push in the same direction. An RtI plan will not work if it is left to individual interpretation of policy, procedure, and instruction.

THE SOLUTION

The global plans of researchers and state agencies are guidelines. It is up the district/school to develop the policies and procedures that will make RtI research come alive at each individual school site. RtI is not a one-size-fits-all recipe that can be replicated at every school. In order to achieve the desired consistency, districts and schools must articulate their individual RtI plans.

> *"In order to achieve the desired consistency, districts and schools must articulate their individual RtI plans…. It means taking global guidelines and turning them into real-life procedures at the district and school sites."*

The purpose of this book is to encourage districts and schools to develop precise plans to ensure quality implementation of an RtI system. Each section identifies a necessary part of the planning process if we are to create a cohesive system of instruction and intervention. It means taking global guidelines and turning them into real-life procedures at the district and school sites. Codifying those policies relieves educators of the guesswork involved when plans are nonspecific.

My final and most vigorous suggestion for designing a successful literacy plan is to develop a handbook that articulates all policies and procedures. The handbook is basically a frequently-asked-

Phase 3

questions document that serves to clarify the process for all stakeholders. It is not a 300-page mammoth that no one will ever reference. It is a short document that specifies policies and procedures outlined in this book. It also serves to articulate mutual-accountability agreements so that all stakeholders are held accountable for their responsibilities in the process. Districts and schools might elect to develop one manual or a series of manuals specific to the stakeholder it references (e.g., individual handbooks might be developed for each intervention tier, for administrators, for teachers, and for parents). The handbook is not written in stone. It is a living document that is revised yearly as new information is discovered and as districts and schools become more sophisticated in implementing an RtI process.

THE WORKSHEET

Worksheet 3.5 is designed to serve as a checklist when developing policies and procedures that will ultimately become your district or school RtI handbook. Although the checklist identifies many common sections needed in the book, your school or district may have additional items to include.

Worksheet 3.5 *The Handbook*

Suggested section	Persons responsible for development	Stakeholder emphasis (teachers, administration, parents)	Completion date
Mission statement			
District/School-Site Literacy RtI Committee contact information			
Awareness sessions—content and schedule			
Assessments required for each tier			
Placement criteria for each tier			
Class configuration for each tier (include who, what, and when)			
Instructional materials and strategies for each tier			
Confirmation of placement procedure			
New student procedure			
Exit criteria for each tier			
Person(s) eligible to teach each tier			
Mutual accountability agreements			
Professional development offerings			
Coaching			
Components of instructional time			
Data collection and analysis			
Grading			
Progress monitoring for students			
Progress monitoring for teachers			
Progress monitoring for administrators			
Working with parents			
Appendix			
▪ Sample weekly lesson plans for each tier			
▪ Pacing plans			
▪ Sample progress reports			
▪ Sample student data-reporting forms			
▪ Sample parent letters in appropriate languages			
▪ Homework idea			
▪ Sample substitute-teacher plans			
▪ Sample student-reporting forms for teachers			

Phase 3

Bibliography

Batsche, G., Elliott, J., Graden, J. L., Grimes, J., Kovaleski, J. G., Prasse, D., Reschly, D., Schrag, J., & Tilly III, D. W. (2007). *Response to intervention: Policy considerations and implementations.* Alexandria, VA: National Association of State Directors of Special Education.

Bender, W. N., & Shores, C. (2007). *Response to intervention: A practical guide for every teacher.* Thousand Oaks, CA: Corwin Press.

Bender Sebring, P., & Bryk, A. (2000, Feburary). School leadership and the bottom line in Chicago. In M. Fullan (2001), *The meaning of educational change.* New York: Teachers College Press.

Biancarosa, G., & Snow, C. (2004). *A vision for action and research in middle and high school literacy: A report to the Carnegie Corporation of New York.* New York: Carnegie Corporation.

Cohen, D. K., & Hill, H. C. (2000, February). *Instructional policy and classroom performance: The mathematics reform in California.* Teachers College Record, *102*(2), 294–393, New York: Teachers College, Columbia University.

Crawford, E., & Torgesen, J. (2007). *Teaching all students to read: Practices from Reading First schools with strong intervention outcomes: Summary Document.* Florida Center for Reading Research. Retrieved July, 2007, from www.fcrr.org/Interventions/pdf/teachingAllStudentsTo ReadSummary.pdf

DuFour, R., Dufour, R., Eaker, R., & Karhanek, G. (2004). *Whatever it takes: How professional learning communities respond when kids don't learn.* Bloomington, IN: National Education Service.

DuFour, R., Eaker, R., & DuFour, R. (Eds.). (2005). *On common ground: The power of professional learning communities.* Bloomington, IN: National Educational Service.

DuFour, R., Dufour, R., Eaker, R., & Many, T. (2006). *Learn by doing: A handbook for professional learning communities at work.* Bloomington, IN: Solution Tree.

Elmore, R. F. (2000). *Building a new structure for school leadership.* Washington, DC: Albert Shanker Institute.

Elmore, R. F. (2002). *Bridging the gap between standards and achievement.* Washington, DC: Albert Shanker Institute.

Elmore, R. F. (2004). *School reform from the inside out: Policy, practice, and performance.* Cambridge, MA: Harvard Education Press.

Fixen, D. L., Naoom, S. F., Blasé, K. A., Friedman, R. M., & Wallace, F. (2005). *Implementation research: A synthesis of the literature.* Tampa, FL: University of South Florida, Louis de la Parte Florida Mental Health Institute, The National Implementation Research Network (FMHI Publication #231).

Foorman, B. R. (2007, May/June). Primary prevention in classroom reading instruction. *Teaching Exceptional Children, 39*(5), 24–30.

Fuchs, L. S., & Fuchs, D. (2007, May/June). A model for implementing responsiveness to intervention. *Teaching Exceptional Children, 39*(5), 14–20.

Fullan, M. (2001). *The new meaning of educational change.* New York: Teachers College Press.

Fullan, M. (2003). *Change forces with a vengeance.* New York: RoutledgeFalmer.

Fullan, M., Hill, P., & Crevola, C. (2006). *Breakthrough.* Thousand Oaks, CA: Corwin Press.

Fullan, M. (2006). *Turnaround leadership.* San Francisco, CA: Jossey-Bass.

Furman, S. H., & Elmore, R. F., (Eds.). (2004). *Redesigning accountability systems for education.* New York: Teachers College Press.

Garmston, R., & Wellman, B. (1999). *The adaptive school: A sourcebook for developing collaborative groups.* Norwood, MA: Christopher-Gordon Publishers, Inc.

Gladwell, M. (2000). *The tipping point.* Boston: Little, Brown, and Company.

Granzin, A. (2006). *Traumatized learning: The emotional consequences of protracted reading difficulties.* Interview by David Boulton for Children of the Code. Retrieved November 19, 2006, from http://www.childrenofthecode.org/interviews/granzin.htm

Hill, P. T., & Celio, M. B. (1998). *Fixing urban schools.* Washington, DC: The Brookings Institution.

Kame'enui, E. J. (2007, May/June). A new paradigm: Responsiveness to intervention. *Teaching Exceptional Children, 39*(5), 6–7.

Kame'enui, E. J., & Simmons, D. C. (2007). *Reading/language arts framework for California public schools.* Sacramento, CA: California Department of Education.

Kame'enui, E. J. (2004). *Differentiated curricula and assessment in reading instruction.* Interview by David Boulton for Children of the Code. Retrieved July 26, 2004, from www.childrenofthecode.org/interviews/kameenui.htm

Lee, J., Grigg, W., & Donahue, P. (2007). *The Nation's Report Card: Reading 2007* (NCES 2007-496). National Center for Education Statistics, Institute of Educational Sciences, U. S. Department of Education, Washington, DC.

Lein, L., Johnson Jr., J. F., & Ragland, M. (1997, February). *Successful Texas schoolwide programs: Research study results.* Austin, TX: University of Texas, Charles A. Dana Center.

Lyon, R. G. (2006). *The federal role in education.* Interview by Nancy Salvato for Education News. Retrieved January 19, 2006, from http://www.educationnews.org

Marzano, R. J., Waters, T., & McNulty, B. A. (2005). *School leadership that works: From research to results.* Aurora, CO: Mid-continent Research for Education and Learning.

McCardle, P., & Chhabra, V. (Eds.). (2004). *The voice of evidence in reading research.* Baltimore, MD: Paul H. Brookes Publishing Co.

McEwan, E. K. (2001). *Raising reading achievement in middle and high schools: 5 simple-to-follow strategies for principals.* Thousand Oaks, CA: Corwin Press, Inc.

Moats, L. C. (2001). When older kids can't read. *Educational Leadership, 58*(6), 36–40.

Moats, L. C. (2007, January). *Whole language high jinks: How to tell when "scientifically based reading instruction" isn't.* Paper written for the Thomas B. Fordham Institute. Retrieved September 29, 2007, from http://www.edexcellence.net/institute/publication/publication.cfm?id=367

National Institute of Child Health and Human Development. (2000). *Report of the national reading panel, teaching children to read: An evidence-based assessment of the scientific research literature on reading and its implications for reading instruction.* Washington, DC: NICHD. (1-800-370-2943).

O'Connor, R. E. (2007). Layers of intervention that affect outcomes in reading. In D. Haager, J. Klingner, & S. Vaughn (Eds.), *Evidenced-based reading practices for response to intervention* (pp.139–157). Baltimore, MD: Paul H. Brookes Publishing Co.

Oxford American Dictionary of Current English. (2002). New York: Oxford University Press (p. 507).

Parker, Christine, Lamb. (2000). Four year old's first test. In B. Smith & K. Judd (Eds.), *Wild sweet notes: Fifty years of West Virginia poetry;1950–1999* (p. 265). Huntington, WV: Publishers Place, Inc.

Pearson, D. P., & Gallagher, M. C. (1983). The instruction of reading comprehension. *Contemporary Educational Psychology,* (8), 317–344.

Perie, M., Grigg, W. S., & Donahue, P. L. (2007). *The nation's report card: Reading 2007 (NCES 2006-451).* U.S. Department of Education, National Center for Education Statistics. Washington, DC: U.S. Government Printing Office.

Reading First. Retrieved August 25, 2007, from http://www.ed.gov/programs/readingfirst/index.html

Reading First Support. Retrieved September 4, 2007, from http://readingfirstsupport.us

Snow-Reiner, R., & Lauer, P. A. (2005). *Professional development analysis.* Denver, CO: Mid-continent Research for Education and Learning.

Torgesen, J. K. (2004). Lessons learned from research on intervention for students who have difficulty learning to read. In P. McCardle & V. Chhabra (Eds.), *The voice of evidence in reading research* (pp. 355–382). Baltimore, MD: Paul H. Brookes Publishing Co.

Torgesen, J. K. (2007). *Using an RTI model to guide early reading instruction: Effects of identification rates for students with learning disabilities.* Florida Center for Reading Research at Florida State University. Retrieved September 27, 2007, from http://www.fcrr.org/science/pdf/torgesen/Response_intervention_Florida.pdf

Vaughn, S. (2003, December). *How many tiers are needed for response to intervention to achieve acceptable prevention outcomes?* Paper presented at the National Research Center on Learning Disabilities Responsiveness to Intervention Symposium, Kansas City, MO.

Walsh, K., Glasser, D., & Wilcox, D. D. (2006). *What education schools aren't teaching about reading and what elementary teacher aren't learning.* (Executive Summary). Washington, DC: National Council on Teacher Quality.